GPS

GPS

Finding Direction on Your Faith and Life Journey

How Luther's Theology Connects Faith to Life

BY JOHN STROMMEN

GPS: FINDING DIRECTION ON YOUR FAITH AND LIFE JOURNEY
How Luther's Theology of Grace and Callings Speaks into the Contemporary
Search for Meaning

Wipf & Stock
An Imprint of Wipf and Stock Publishers
199 W. 8th Ave., Suite 3
Eugene, OR 97401

www.wipfandstock.com

PAPERBACK ISBN: 978-1-6667-8146-5
HARDCOVER ISBN: 978-1-6667-8147-2
EBOOK ISBN: 978-1-6667-8148-9

I dedicate this book to the memory of
Merton and Irene, my father and mother,
who taught me that being a Christian wasn't
agreeing with propositions about God, but
living in a relationship with God.

Man's constant mistake is that he thinks he is doing something by himself.

—*Gustaf Wingren, Luther on Vocation*

CONTENTS

FOREWORD

Once in a great while, a mature and experienced pastor who could have chosen to do doctoral work immediately following seminary classes chooses to return to the graduate classroom at the height of his pastoral experience. This study book represents both a sophisticated philosophical and theological perspective with a deeply complex and effective pastoral experience. Needless to say, a rare document. For that reason alone, it should be used in congregations.

The subject matter is both urgent, timely, and profoundly needed. Any assessment of Christian local churches in European-centered Christianity finds a profound challenge. In part, this challenge is the great disjunction between contemporary culture and the predominant culture of the local church. For the everyday people in the pew, this disjunction is often experienced as little or no connection between their Sunday faith and their Monday through Saturday lives. Increasingly the general culture gives less and less public space and time for faith and its public expressions. The disjunction is even greater for the person who is socially unrelated to a local church. Either from within or without the disjunction reveals itself as a great existential challenge.

Following the work of Martin Luther, Douglas John Hall, Carl Braaten and others, this study book recognizes the profound challenges of postmodernity and does not propose quick fixes. Indeed, part of the argument takes seriously Hall's recommendation that we wait patiently and await the clarity that comes in a theology of the cross. This study book takes its start with theological anthropology and the theology of the cross, with a posture of humility and listening. However, it does not begin in silence and resignation but rather with a humble, confident witness.

The study book uses the two foci of justification and vocation to formulate both the challenge facing the lives of contemporary postmoderns and the shape of an appropriate way of joining the gospel to this contemporary challenge. This use of the doctrine of justification and vocation in the manner the study does is remarkably fresh and promising. Integrating this profound pairing of Reformation thought to a missional ecclesiology truly reveals how integrated the thought of the argument is.

I especially appreciate the use of various media for exploring the experience of justification and vocation in contemporary North American society and culture. The use of film is in itself a sufficient reason to use this study book in local church life.

Patrick R. Keifert

PREFACE

Why did I write *GPS: Finding Direction on Your Faith and Life Journey*? Allow me to answer by way of a story. As a church youth director on a backpacking trip in Wyoming, I recall a short hike we took through the forest to a lake to go fishing. There was no path, but we managed to find our way. The return trip did not go as smoothly. Thinking it would be a snap to return to our campsite, we set out, making our way through the woods. We were quite certain we were headed in the right direction, and yet nothing seemed familiar. Eventually, after forty-five minutes or so, expecting to arrive back at our campsite, we stumbled upon something quite unexpected: the very same shoreline of the lake we had left forty-five minutes earlier! Which, in retrospect, was very, very fortunate, because we were lost and didn't know it! Thinking we were headed in a straight line, we had in fact gone in a circle. My questionable leadership and deplorable navigational skills aside, we dejectedly became aware that the last forty-five minutes were nothing more than pointless meandering. I didn't have access to GPS in those days, but a simple compass would have been helpful.

The truth is, an increasing number of people today feel that their lives are pointless, akin to going in circles or repeating the same endless routine, day after day, with no meaningful direction. Erich Fromm once wrote that "man is the only animal for whom his existence is a problem which he has to solve."[1] Simply put, unlike our fellow creatures, we know we are going to die, and, with that in mind, we ponder the significance and meaning of our individual existence. *Why* have I been put on this planet? Does *anything* I do matter? Do *I* matter? And, as Fromm suggested, we must solve these questions in a satisfactory way. Failure to do so leaves us not knowing *where* we are, *why* we are, and *what direction* we're supposed to go—all of which is the very essence of being lost. And with it, I might add, come loss of hope and a sustaining sense of meaning.

As a pastor I have listened to countless people trying to make sense of their lives, to solve their existence, if you will. It seems that the greatest goal of many people is for themselves and their loved ones to be happy. After all, what could be more American than "the pursuit of happiness"?[2] But here is where we get stuck in an existential quagmire. For we humans, happiness is exceedingly elusive without such assets as a clear identity and purpose. And, sad to say, happiness in itself is more by-product than valid purpose. Nor is achieving success, accumulating wealth, or creating our own identity. Nothing more than rearranging the deck furniture on the Titanic.

Given that a majority of human beings do believe in God, it would seem that they could call upon God to help them with their bearings, to establish a sense of meaning and direction. And yet it is an existential consequence of the modern age that people generally feel that God is distant and without agency in their lives. The bottom line is that without the sense that there is a God who is invested in our daily world (and in *me*) and that what I do with my time matters, the human animal is left with an impoverished soul. And so, we wander.

That is why I wrote this book, to help people of faith *connect their faith* to their daily existence, so that this life (not just their *next* life) could have meaning and purpose. Hence, in the pages that follow I will encourage you to carefully reflect on the God who calls you to abundant life and meaningful engagement with the world that utilizes your unique and particular gifts. While actual GPS technology can only provide us with information, this book is about being the receiver and giver of the gift of transcendent love. It is just such a love that establishes the coordinates for the purpose, meaning, and direction of our lives. One could call it *GPS: God's Promises Synchronizing*. Kind of a mouthful, yes, but it is nonetheless true that a biblical faith holds to the truth that God has promised to continue

---

1   "Erich Fromm Quotes."
2   "Extract from Declaration," line 2.

creating, preserving, and transforming life. We are first recipients, but also partners in that promise! And promise creates a life-giving sense of meaning and hopefulness for the future and in our advance toward it.

As a pastor, I have learned over and over again that the connection of God and faith to life cannot be assumed with anyone. In one church I was serving, I remember grabbing a burger and a beer with a lay leader in the congregation whom I will refer to as Bob. During our conversation, I alluded to his calling from God as an architect. He was incredulous. "I don't have a calling," he responded. "*You* have a calling. You're a pastor. I just have a job to make a living." As his pastor, I reminded him what Luther taught long ago, namely, that all people of faith have callings, whether within the church or as an architect, teacher, lawyer, mechanic, business-person, parent, or friend. And the list goes on and on, corresponding with all the spaces and places where we live and work—what Luther referred to as one's "stations"[3] of life. Luther believed that it is precisely in those places that the relevance of the Ten Commandments kicks in; it is here that God calls us to love our neighbor and work to make the world a better, more loving, and more *God-aware* place. And we do it through our callings, or as Luther called it, "vocations."[4]

When Bob pointed out to me that no one in our congregation believes their daily work is a calling, it dawned on me: as pastors, we've done a lousy job teaching Luther's wonderful doctrine of "the priesthood of all believers."[5] Well, at least I've done a lousy job, anyway! For Luther, all baptized members of the body of Christ are called to be participants in God's ongoing and all-encompassing mission to this broken world, thus making up a vast community of folks ordained for God's work—hence, *priests*, of a sort. Indeed, there is no shortage of ways that people of faith—or any well-meaning person, for that matter—can proactively love their neighbor and make a difference in the world, however modest or mundane it may be.

Not only do we all have callings from God, God is already at work in the places where we live and work, beckoning us to partner with God in the task of protecting and nourishing life in all its manifestations! Hence, Luther believed that "Man's constant mistake is that he thinks he is do-ing something by himself."[6] As theologian Gustaf Wingren notes, "God dwells in heaven, but he lives and works on earth,"[7] and wants people as

---

3 Wingren, *Luther on Vocation*, 17.
4 Wingren, *Luther on Vocation*, 5.
5 Gritsch and Jenson, *Lutheranism*, 111.
6 Wingren, *Vocation*, 135.
7 Wingren, *Vocation*, 123.

his fellow workers. Whether any of us know it or not, we are instruments and coworkers with God![8]

The importance of Luther's vocational theology cannot be underestimated, but its foundation is often overlooked: that would be justification. Luther's most famous doctrine is *justification by grace through faith,* and this is the real game changer, for it is God's justification of us that *frees* us and *empowers* us to do vocation, to respond to our callings. Without God's justification, we are lost in our desperate attempts at self-justification and we are not free to love our neighbor. It is my hope that in the following pages, we might be prompted to reflect and act on the good news that we have been set free by God's justification of us to be our true, authentic, and best selves. Which is to say, our most grateful and loving selves, anchored in the trust that God will provide *for* me and *through* me for my neighbor.

As a Lutheran pastor and theologian, my reflections are from an unapologetically Lutheran perspective, but I hope that does not discourage all the non-Lutherans out there to read this! While recognizing my dependence on Luther's thought, I would also invite you to consider that Luther laid down the core principles of the entire Protestant Reformation. Hence, many of us—Lutherans and non-Lutherans alike—already live and breathe in his theological wake. And so, it comes to this: in light of the existential struggles of many modern and postmodern human beings, I have come to believe more powerfully every day that the core insights of Luther into scripture, tradition, and experience are as valid today —possibly more so—than even 500 years ago. As a people who struggle terribly with our sense of self and an increasingly elusive sense of hopeful meaning to our lives, the twin theological pillars of *justification* by grace through faith and *vocation* as a calling are not only relevant today, they are precisely the good news we long to hear!

---

8 Wingren, *Vocation,* 134.

INTRODUCTION

As many have already observed, Christian belief and practice in the Western world faces significant challenges in the present postmodern era. Thanks to the legacy of the Enlightenment, the marginalization of the idea of God by so-called enlightened human beings has been subsequently embedded in our culture. Meanwhile, our estimation of human potential has skyrocketed. After all, with science at our disposal, we've figured out many of the secrets of the natural world. Or so we believe. And it's gone to our heads! According to this modern narrative, we can become masters of the universe, and hence, our own destinies. Meanwhile, God has been relegated to the sidelines with the advent of Deism—the belief that God set everything in motion and now sits back in the bleachers, uninvolved, as the game of history plays itself out. Or, even worse, we don't even need God in the equation at all. After all, the thinking goes, we need to put childish notions aside and grow up.

As a result of the massive and shifting assumptions about God, people generally feel free of the sort of guilt that haunted Luther and his contemporaries as they fretted over their justification before a harshly judgmental God. In the sixteenth century the meaning of life was filled with cosmic urgency: make sure you're on the track toward heaven and beware the wide path to hell! And no one needed reminding that according to Roman

Catholic theology, one's justification before God relied partly on human agency (God did his part, now you must do yours). Luther's revolutionary move, born out of revisiting scripture and tradition, was to posit that God and God alone justifies us as pure gift through no effort of our own. The alternative is endless preoccupation with self and self-interest.

We modern folk, in contrast to pre-moderns, view God as far less judgmental—not necessarily because we've accepted Luther's teaching that God justifies us, but because we tend to believe God is either too distant, too disinterested, or too *nonexistent* to give us grades anymore. To the extent we believe God *is* interested in us, we make God dance to the tune of our culture (or at least we try!) as we domesticate and commodify God as a resource for our self-realization. Consequently, we encourage people to shop for a church that features a God we like, or we accessorize God as an on-call therapist to occasionally help us smooth out the rough patches in life.[1] Needless to say, there is unprecedented freedom for the modern and postmodern person to determine their own identity, meaning, and destiny.

And that freedom is killing us! Our attempts to create our own meaning and identity *ex nihilo* (out of nothing) are merely updated attempts to justify ourselves and become our own gods. But left with results that can best be described as hollow and unsatisfactory, we have realized that we don't handle the role of God very well,[2] and the future suddenly looks radically different and far less hopeful. So, rather than experiencing guilt, modern folk are plagued by an oppressive sense of meaninglessness—and its ever-present companion, hopelessness—that easily leads to depression, addictions, and just plain emptiness.[3] These modern folk include people of faith who may believe in the Christian story but breathe the air of modern culture every day—air that leaves the human spirit gasping for something redemptive and transcendent.

GPS was born out of the conviction that people of faith want to connect their faith to their lives in meaningful ways but don't know how. Simply put, as creatures of postmodernity, we lack the imaginations to visualize what that means. As a result, faith tends not to be a relationship with the living God that animates our lives and fills it with meaning, but rather a set of propositions about an abstract God. Christian faith has thus been reduced to the sterile confines of our cognition, rather than the dynamic

---

1 Zscheile, *Agile Church*, 25.
2 Braaten, *Principles*, 69.
3 Hall, *Context*, 131.

relationship between God and believer suggested by the biblical world-view. This leaves us with a crisis of meaning in our daily lives.

To address this modern crisis, one must begin with God, not self. When we think it all begins with us, we will be like Narcissus staring too intently at his reflection in the water. Our purpose and meaning, therefore, do not begin with gift assessments or goals we set for ourselves, but with questions about God: Who is God? How does God regard me? What is God up to in this world? Only when we begin with God and God's life-giving mission to the world through Jesus, can we meaningfully ask, How am I a part of what God is up to? Purpose, meaning, and hope for us come directly from our relationship with God, from the rhythm of God at work in the world, and from our partnership with God in that very work.

It is only through a trusting relationship with God that we realize that all the things that are most important in life—wholeness, forgiveness, faith, hope, love, meaning, purpose, life itself, and *new* life in Christ—are pure gifts from our maker and redeemer, not things we create for ourselves. Theologian Oswald Bayer has suggested that living in a state of dependence on God for such gifts is what it means to be human.[4] We are creatures that receive life and new life—and all that makes life worth living—from God and through no effort of our own. Echoing scripture, Luther reminds us that all these gracious gifts are given in order to create trust in God's providence for us and turn us toward our neighbor in servanthood and love. This is God's calling for all created human beings, but in failing to trust God, turning in on ourselves and away from our neighbor, we have created a fallen world to which we are captive.

But in the new—and second—creation, Christ frees us from our captivity to a stunted humanity with the unconditional promise of a new self, restored to a trusting relationship with God and the capacity to love our neighbor. This is our justification, and it comes solely from Christ. With the dawn of this new creation, we are freed from fretting over our existential status and fragile identity in this world; freed to embody a love not merely based on feelings, but on a Spirit committed to my neighbors' well-being; freed to co-create a more trustworthy world with God and bear witness to a new and promised world. God's Promises Synchronizing.

With these two creations, we have the entire Judeo-Christian tradition and its unfolding story, and the basis for Parts I and II. In the first creation—as the Ten Commandments make clear—we are called to love God

---

4 Bayer, *Luther's Theology*, 98-100.

and neighbor. Hence, the giftedness of creation clearly is not intended for me alone, but for my neighbor as well. Luther's explanation of the first article of the Apostle's Creed beautifully identifies the many—and unmerited—gifts God has given to us, including our bodies and minds; clothing, and shelter; food, drink, and the natural world; our families, communities, and livelihood.[5] And the Commandments make clear that our lives are to be lived in *proactive* love for God and neighbor—not merely avoiding violations of our neighbor but engaging in their nurture. The Apostle's Creed spells out the spirit in which our servanthood is carried out: as recipients of body and mind, clothing and shelter, food, drink, families, and livelihood, we are right to give God thanks and praise. And this spirit of gratitude is vital because a grateful heart is one that seeks to ensure that *all* may have sound body and mind, clothing, shelter, and so on.

Indeed, the many gifts we've each been given are signs not only of the loving care with which our creator has made us but also signs of how we are called. In the economy of God's love, we pass on the life we receive; we do not hoard it. We are members of a community of creation, where we are not merely members of a diverse human family but where, as St. Francis taught us, we have brothers and sisters of different species as well. All of this is to say that we are continually called back to the words from the book of Genesis, namely, to *till and keep* the garden—the community of life that is creation itself. And so indeed, the love one receives from God is for the purpose of creating abundant life in that person, yet it is never intended to stop with them, but to be channeled to their neighbor and community writ large.

Since this creation has been distorted by human rebellion against God's purposes, God has also graciously given us the law (Ten Commandments) to turn us back to God, restrain sin, and help human beings to thrive. But we are not alone with God's commands, for God has given God's own self to creation in all its facets—natural, public, private—while actively working within this world so that all life may flourish. It is good news in its own right that all human beings, regardless of their beliefs, are called to partner with God in the world to be "co-creators of a more trustworthy world"[6]—and a more loving, God-centered one. Luther even said that it is God himself who milks the cows through the person whose vocation that is![7]

This is good news because it means that what we do in this broken world matters, even in the mundane, everyday moments of life as we know it.

---

5 Kolb and Wengert, *Book of Concord*, 354.
6 Keifert, *Talking*, 31.
7 Luther quoted in Wingren, *Vocation*, 9.

That God's good and gracious gifts are simultaneously for our own pleasure and growth as well as my neighbor's benefit makes life meaningful. For instance, the gift and capacity for empathy deeply enriches the life of the empathizer through a closer sense of community and mutuality. But that same person's empathy gives particularity to their sense of calling, as they are uniquely suited to give encouragement and life to *someone who needs* precisely that very thing: the knowledge that one is connected to someone who cares; that one is not alone with their struggles.

So it is that we are partners with God as curators of an ongoing creation, whose purpose is the thriving and flourishing of life in its many and various forms (remember our charter in Genesis). Hence, God invites us to consider our uniqueness as individuals, in the gifts we've been given, in order to find clues about how God calls us to work in the world and let the gifts which we've been given become generative. In this course, we will explore a broad set of gifts that begin with the places, roles, and relationships that constitute our daily lives to the life story that is our own. But the gifts go on to include the values and passions that guide us, as well as our personality and natural abilities.

What we will not cover in this book are financial and material gifts. Fortunately, the topic of financial stewardship has been written about very extensively, so there is no lack of reflection here. We will focus, rather, on the gifts that are manifest in relationships, narratives, and personhood, and how they can be used in the service of love for our neighbor and creation.

There is a massive problem in our world, however, that undermines the move from self to neighbor, and it leads to the second creation. Instead of trusting God, our world in all of its folly urges people to trust in whatever slice of creation they can possess, to "Get what you can while you can." In other words, live for yourself or your tribe (ultimately, an extension of self). The human rebellion called sin ensnares us in a hopeless preoccupation with self as we seek to create our own purpose and meaning—indeed, our own justification. Hence, my neighbor will generally benefit from me when it is also—and not by accident—in my self-interest. "The self seeks its own self in all things, even in its piety. There is no way out."[8] In other words, our love often isn't really love, but feelings tethered to self-interest, as we are strongly inclined to love that which pleases us. Even when we mean well, it always comes back to me. And this inward curve does not foster life; it diminishes life and ultimately destroys it. The meaning we seek to

---

8 Forde, *Theologian of the Cross*, 54.

create does not sustain us or our neighbor and, as a result, the prospects for our sense of a collective future crumble. When our self-justification becomes embedded in society's infrastructure, institutions, and culture, our problems only intensify.

"Who will save me from this body that is carrying me to death" (Rom 7:24)?

Only a new creation brought into being from the one who is continually creating anew can save us from ourselves. Jesus the Christ, God incarnate, is the new creation into which we are invited—a rebirth into a new future that only God can give and we can only receive in faith. This new creation, however, is as much about death as it is about life—the death of a humanity hopelessly distorted by sin. This twofold movement of death and life is best expressed through the theological lens Luther spoke of as *theologia crucis*, "theology of the cross."[9] *Theologia crucis* makes it clear that the drama of Jesus's death and life is all about two creations, namely, the death of a fallen and distorted one and the birth of a new creation bearing the fullness of God's promise of abundant life. This means that Jesus's death is ours as well—the death of the very pretense and self-righteousness that lurks in us all that put Jesus on the cross! And, it must be said, the death of the very possibility of us self-correcting out of our rebellion, for we are too far down the rabbit hole to save ourselves. By taking on the weight of our dysfunctional and doomed humanity while extending to those same humans the life and community of God's own self, God in Jesus has restored our relationship of trust in our creator and rekindled hope. Grounded in a right relationship with God—the very meaning of justification—we are freed from our own attempts at self-justification and from the very forces that prevent us from living an abundant life, loving our neighbor, and partnering with God.

It cannot be stressed enough that God's justification of his wayward creatures is *precisely* what frees us to love our neighbor and engage in meaningful work with God, for *only* God's unconditional promise of new life and community can release us from our self-serving agendas, self-justifying ways, and general preoccupation with self. This twofold dance is the very dance of justification and vocation. As recipients of life *and* new life, we are turned to our neighbor to be agents of the very same life and new life. Our agency is secondary, however, as we now channel a love and a goodness that we neither create nor possess. It comes from God and we cling to it in faith and servanthood. And so it is that the promise of God's kingdom to come is intended not just to give us hope, but to be

---

9 Hall, *Cross in Context*, 6.

generative—passed on to others as good news. Just as Christ bears our burdens for us and welcomes us into the life of God, we, too, help our neighbor bear their burdens and proclaim to them the promises of God that give life. Just as I am forgiven, I, too, forgive.

We begin our journey, however, in the first creation where God calls us to be stewards who till and keep the garden of creation. Each chapter will focus on a gift that is given by God and how that gift *pivots* into a calling and a way for us to love our neighbor. Appropriately, Part I is entitled: Co-creating a trustworthy world with God.

In Chapter 1, we will unpack the gift of *meaning*. In a world plagued by the experience of meaninglessness and loneliness, we assert that God is radically present and active in the world, infusing it with meaning, purpose, and life-giving community. We are then called to participate with God in God's activity and purpose.

In Chapter 2, we examine the gift of the very *places* we live our life. In these places of life, we are given roles to embody and people with whom we can establish meaningful relationships. Such roles as parent, coworker, and friend are among the highest of callings.

In Chapter 3, we consider the gift of *your story*. The story that makes up each of our lives is—or can be—a blessing to us, even the difficult chapters. A theology of the cross reminds us that God's story intertwines with ours in an act of solidarity and redemption, shaping our own story to be a blessing to our neighbor.

In Chapter 4, we unpack the gift of your *passions* and *values*. For each of us, the fire in the belly that inspires us in tandem with the values that guide us can be a compass that guides us to align with God's purposes and get to work!

In Chapter 5, we explore the gift of your *personality*. Your unique being and presence is a gift you bring to the world that allows God to work through you in very specific ways.

In Chapter 6, we examine the gift of your *natural abilities*. All of us are endowed with life gifts that make us good at certain things. It is God's intention to utilize our gifts for the sake of making the world a better place.

In the re-creation, or second creation, God's love goes unfathomably deeper, and with it, the gifts we receive. Through the life, death, and resurrection of Jesus Christ, God has destroyed the ultimate power of sin, death, and the forces of evil so that we can have abundant life. In a world doomed by unmet conditions, God's Word of unconditional promise creates a new world where we, in all our brokenness, are grafted in as members. How, one might ask? Through baptism into Christ's own self—an inclusion that is pure grace, gift, and promise. This amounts to nothing less than participation in the life of the eternal God and the restoration of abundant life that will come to full fruition in God's own time. The gifts of forgiveness, new creation, and reconciliation with God are simultaneously callings as well, for our giftedness is both a reminder of God's providence and grace as well as a commission to partner with God in proclaiming the good news of God's promises. And so, we move on to Part II, entitled: Living in the promise of the new creation in Christ.

Part II begins with Chapter 7 and *the hope and promise of a new creation*. As created beings, we are gifted with a creation to care for but have failed to do so! As we muddle along in this broken world, we are keenly aware that things are not what they are supposed to be. Human intuition and scripture both paint a vivid picture of what God's kingdom looks like—the very answer to our existential plight.

In Chapter 8, we take a careful look at the gift of a *new self in Christ*. In baptism, we are reborn as members of the body of Christ, called to be Christ in the world and bear our neighbors' broken humanity just as Christ has borne ours.

In Chapter 9, we explore the gifts *for building up the church*. As members of the body of Christ, the gift of the Holy Spirit is given to us, subsequently equipping each of us with gifts for the purpose of building up the body of Christ.

In Chapter 10, we open up the gift of the *freedom to be you*. The unconditional promises of God justify us and disarm all forms of brokenness. We are then free to authentically be ourselves and do what we were meant to do: live life abundantly and love our neighbor.

In Chapter 11, we examine the gift of hope found in the *kingdom of God*—the new creation. The main thing that we Christians do is bear witness to the promise that God's vision for humanity will one day come to fruition. Out of the hope engendered by this promise, we point to, advocate for, and practice kingdom values in our lives.

In Chapter 12, we take a careful look at the gift of *partners*: God and people. Our callings must be tended to by gathering with others in the community of faith to encourage, guide, support, and, most of all, turn us toward the one who calls us. We also learn that God calls us to a broader community in our neighborhoods, to both discover God's presence there and serve God's purposes.

Throughout the book I will make us of narrative excerpts from films that offer illustrations of the themes we are discussing. I believe that theology gets played out as much in life stories and fiction as it does in sanctuaries. After all, if God is present and at work in the everyday world, it stands to reason that the dramas around us can be our classroom.

Weekly rhythm of the coursework

This book is written for either use in private study and reflection or in a group/class format. A combination of both of these is probably best, as previous participants have found great value in reading and reflecting, followed by engaging in community-building conversation with others. Doing the advance work and reflection greatly enhances the group conversation, rather than trying to digest the material for the first time in a class and then taking time to journal when that time could be used for conversation.

If you are working through GPS by yourself, I encourage you to pause after each chapter to reflect, write, and live with it for a few days before moving on to the next chapter. If one prefers to knock down several chapters at a time, that's fine, too, as long as you don't omit time to reflect!

Above all, I invite you to open your mind for critical reflection on your place in God's story, open your heart to engage in new possibilities for loving servanthood, and open your spirit to the presence of the God of love in Christ Jesus.

ACKNOWLEDGMENTS

No book is ever the work of just one person, but, rather, a team that allows an author to write with confidence. I would like to thank some of those people now.

I want to thank Matthew Wimer, my editor with Wipf and Stock Publishers, for his gracious flexibility with a first-time author who needed extra time navigating the publishing process. Many thanks to Wipf and Stock for giving me this opportunity to share my work with a broader audience.

I am grateful to Jenni Lathrop, graphic designer extraordinaire, both for her skill and the patience of Job through my countless edits and revisions. As Jenni now knows, pastors (like me) who edit sermons right up to the last second often do the same if they are working on a book!

Members of Mt. Carmel Lutheran Church of Minneapolis constituted the first class I taught using the GPS material. Their enthusiasm and honest feedback were an immense help to me as I was still ironing out the content and shape of the book. Among other things, they helped me to see the importance of the gift of conversation partners that only enhanced our reflection experiences with GPS.

I will always be filled with thanks for the good people of Mt. Olivet Lutheran Church of Plymouth, Minnesota, where I served as senior pastor for twenty-plus years. They were my theological partners on a journey of discovery as we sought to understand and practice what mission looks like in the twenty-first century. So many of our shared experiences are woven into my book.

Dr. Mark Tranvik, professor of Reformation history and theology at Luther Seminary, read early drafts of my book and has been a steadfast advocate throughout my writing process. Mark has written insightfully on the topic of Luther's doctrine of vocation, so I treasure his encouragement and helpful feedback.

I am grateful to Dr. Roland Martinson, former dean and professor emeritus of Luther Seminary, for our long-standing relationship. Rollie has essentially been my pastor for my adult life, helping me to weave life, callings, and theology into a life-giving narrative that has contributed greatly to this book.

I am deeply indebted to Dr. Patrick Keifert, professor emeritus of systematic theology at Luther Seminary and the founder of Church Innovations Institute, where I served on the board for many years. Pat is my theological mentor and one of the most brilliant theologians I have known. Pat was my academic adviser when I launched the GPS project as an independent study at Luther Seminary. Since then, he has completed deep and substantive reviews of my material in preparation for publishing and has been a strong advocate of my work.

My brother Peter, a longtime Lutheran pastor and former bishop, has provided encouragement and thoughtful feedback throughout my writing process. The camaraderie we share around exploring the depths of Lutheran missional theology is very meaningful to me.

Last, and most importantly, I want to thank my wife, Heidi, whose supportive spirit (and continued employment!) has allowed me to retire a couple of years early and write. I am most fortunate to have a partner like her in life—and in my callings. Such fortune is a reminder of the magnitude of unmerited gifts we receive from God—the gift of the ones we love most.

LIST OF ABBREVIATIONS

Gen. . . . . Genesis

2 Cor. 2 Corinthians

Phil . . . . Philippians

Eph . . . . Ephesians

Exod . . . . Exodus

Rev . . . . Revelation

Isa . . . . Isaiah

Col . . . . Colossians

Rom . . . . Romans

Heb. . . . . Hebrews

Eccl. . . . . Ecclesiastes

PART I

Co-creating a Trustworthy World with God

Work is not primarily a thing one does to live
but the thing one lives to do.

—*Dorothy Sayers, "Why Work?"*

CHAPTER 1

THE GIFT OF MEANING

CHAPTER OVERVIEW

In this first chapter, we begin with the ebb and flow of everyday life and how we experience it. Indeed, this is precisely where faith must be lived out to be meaningful. As we reflect on our daily existence, we examine the modern plight of meaninglessness and how it is rooted in a collective imagination that excludes God from this world. This exclusion leads to three distinctly different but powerful expressions of meaninglessness: daily lives that are busy but seem pointless, futile attempts to create meaning for ourselves, and a haunting disconnect from our neighbors that leaves us feeling our relationships are without meaning. It must be noted that a close companion of meaning—or lack of it—is hope. To address a meaningful life is to address a hopeful one, too, as we shall see more clearly in Chapter 11.

I hope you will come to see that a genuine sense of meaning is founded upon three essential things:

1. Our world and our lives are filled with the active presence of God.
2. God calls us to partner with God to co-create a more trustworthy and hopeful world.

3. A relationship with God is never merely private, but participation in a community.

Introduction to the gift of meaning

FILM CLIP
In the 1977 film, *Annie Hall*, the modern plight of meaning-lessness is depicted in a truthful, yet humorous way. Young schoolboy Alvy Singer is growing up in Brooklyn in the 1940s. He has stopped studying because he is disturbed by the modern suggestion among scientists that one day the ever-expanding universe will simply fall apart. When his mother wants to know what that has to do with Alvy not doing his homework, he responds with perfect comedic deadpan: "What's the point?" And so, bright but troubled little Alvy Singer has channeled the very question fueled by the modern existential crisis of a godless, mechanistic universe. *What's the point?*[1]

Reflection and conversation: What is it like to live in my skin?

Since this book is intended to address your lived-in everyday life, that is where we must begin. While *Annie Hall* appropriately makes light of the modern bias of a godless, material universe, it is highly relevant that the God of Christian faith addresses and encounters each of us in the context of our regular, daily existence. Take a few minutes to journal about what a typical day looks like for you. Then reflect on the meaning—or lack of meaning—in that experience. Part of that reflection will include considering whether or not you experience God as part of your everyday world.

Please begin by constructing a schedule of a typical weekday for you:

6 a.m. _____

7 a.m. _____

8 a.m. _____

9 a.m. _____

---

1   Allen, *Annie Hall*, 2:33–3:18.

10 a.m. _____

11 a.m. _____

Noon _____

1 p.m. _____

2 p.m. _____

3 p.m. _____

4 p.m. _____

5 p.m. _____

6 p.m. _____

7 p.m. _____

8 p.m. _____

9 p.m. _____

10 p.m. _____

11 p.m. _____

REFLECT ON THE SCHEDULE OF YOUR TYPICAL DAY:

What does it feel like at the end of the day? Choose one word to summarize.

_____

What did I accomplish? For whom?

_____

_____

_____

Does my daily activity matter? To whom?

_____

_____

_____

Pick a random time during your schedule. What was God doing at that time?

_____

_____

_____

Is your faith in God connected to your everyday life in a meaningful way? If so, how? If not, why not?

_____

_____

_____

LEARNING: A CRISIS OF MEANING

While most of us believe in God, many are commonly plagued by "practical atheism,"[2] a major source of the feeling of meaninglessness. Practical atheism means believing in God but living as though there were no God. It's not anyone's fault. It has more to do with limitations on our imaginations and how we talk about God—largely imposed by modern Western culture and the Enlightenment. For better or worse, for most of human history people believed God was near and the world was alive with spiritual presence. Everything one did mattered because God was both watching and participating in a world that hosted a struggle between good and evil. In a secular age like ours, God and spiritual presences have been stripped away from our narrative framework and the result is just you and me and a demythologized, flat world. And one without apparent meaning.

---

2 Keifert, *Here Now*, 62.

What follows are three fundamental ways we experience meaninglessness, especially as practical atheists. And closely following a loss of meaning is any sense of hope for the future.

The three faces of meaninglessness

The first way the absence of God is felt is in the pervasive sense that daily life is an empty juggling act, that life is just one *&^%$#@ thing after another and lacks meaningful purpose. For many, our days consist of just trying to get through everything! The myth of Sisyphus is relevant here. According to this ancient myth, Sisyphus tirelessly pushes a boulder up a hill, only to have it roll down when he reaches the top—so he has to push it right back up again, day after day. In a Sisyphean world, one's existence and the world itself seem to be irredeemably pointless, and, let's just say it: Godless. This aptly describes the experience of many today.[3] And amid our many efforts to hold our responsibilities together and honor our obligations, we ask, "What's the point?" If the future holds no point, no purpose, and no promise for us, our capacity to hope for a better future quickly vanishes.

A second way meaninglessness is manifest in our lives follows from the first. In a world void of clear meaning, we feel the need to create meaning for ourselves but suffer from the painful realization that we cannot. As Luther might put it, we feel the need to justify our existence. This is reflected in the very modern and existential question: "How do you justify taking up time and space?" In a world where we are urged to win friends and influence people, how do we stack up? The pressure is on to create meaning and value for ourselves somehow, to make a name for ourselves, establish a "brand," and create our own story and identity.[4] But our attempts do not succeed. We can never get there. We are haunted by the feeling that our own worth is suspect, and furthermore, we are doubtful that we make much of a difference in the world. This quest for the advancement of self is a unique by-product of our assumption—courtesy of the age of science and reason—that with our new tools and knowledge, we can solve any problem. This only makes the realization that we *can't* solve all of our problems—particularly the most important ones—even more discouraging. A lack of hope in a positive outcome then breeds a sense of meaninglessness.

Third, the absence of God produces a lonelier universe, where, in trying to fill the void by making our own meaning, we inevitably focus too much

3 Hall, *The Cross*, 129-31
4 Bayer, *Luther's Theology*, 97-102.

on self, as the classic doctrine of sin as *incurvatus se* dictates. *Incurvatus se* is a Latin term that means curving in on oneself and away from God and other people. This results in a world where we are increasingly alienated from meaningful relationships and community, as countless studies suggest about modern Western culture. As a result, more than ever before, people today often feel that their lives are disconnected, that they are not meaningfully connected to others in a life-giving way.[5] Ironically, in a time when so many social media options and opportunities are open to us, many feel alone and unable to connect beyond superficial ways. Without a solid sense of belonging, life loses meaning quickly. In isolation, we become radically *less* hopeful creatures as well. This is made all the more poignant when the very creation of a powerful social media platform is unable to quell the loneliness one may feel, as the following film excerpt illustrates.

FILM CLIP

In the 2010 film, *The Social Network*, we learn the story of the creation of Facebook. While this revolutionary development links people everywhere in exciting and new ways, it also has the capacity to ironically make people lonelier, substituting brief technological interactions for real community. In the final scene of the movie, Mark Zuckerberg (played by Jesse Eisenberg), the creator of Facebook, channels the alienating potential of this movement as he stares into his computer screen, waiting for a reply to his friend request to a former girlfriend he regrets losing. Ironically, he lost her because he didn't have time for her while developing social media to bring people closer together. More broadly, it represents the search for the authentic human connection that eludes him now.[6]

God's response to our crisis of meaning

THE GOD WHO IS PRESENT AND INVESTED

Modern humans make the tragic mistake of thinking it falls upon us to create meaning and identity for ourselves. And yet, as finite creatures, this is futile without beginning with God. Creating such life-giving forces as meaning and purpose or to discover something as profound and basic as identity is impossible within the confines of our own selves.[7] These things

5 Elton, *Journeying*, 82-87.
6 Fincher, *Social Network*, 1:53:45–1:55:35.
7 Kolb, *Genius*, 38.

are gifts only realized out of our relationship with the one who made us. The good news for us—as Christian theology teaches—is that God seeks to cultivate a relationship with us because God loves us and is invested in life that is whole and thriving.

In response to the feeling that God is absent from our world, I contend that God is very much present. The world God made is a gift to us that is filled with meaning because God is present and at work there, publicly and privately. After all, God made the world, and despite its compromised nature, God loves God's creation and is at work in both church and world creating and recreating, sustaining and redeeming, restoring and trans-forming. The world and our lives are then unfolding toward a hopeful end.

Consider the power of the Apostle Paul's description of God's presence with us: "Though indeed he is not far from each one of us. For 'In Him, we live and move and have our being'," (Acts 17:27–28).

Or remember the proclamation in John's Gospel that Christ is the means through which all things were made: "All things came into being through him, and without him not one thing came into being" (John 1:3).

Ponder the rich language describing the total investment that God has made in creation and in us: "I will pour out my Spirit upon all flesh" (Acts 2:17).

And, of course, there is no more profound statement of how God regards the created world than the incarnation of Christ in Jesus of Nazareth. Particularly for Luther, the Word becoming flesh is far more than a one-off to forgive our sins. Christ has taken up residence on earth and in human affairs! Furthermore, the incarnation of Christ is a sign that God has taken the created order—even humanity itself—*into God's own self*. In Christ, we see God's total solidarity with and presence in creation.

THE GOD WHO CREATES MEANING AND PURPOSE

In response to the second manifestation of meaninglessness—the cul-turally reinforced task of justifying your existence by creating your own worth—I counter that it is God alone who justifies, and establishes our worth and identity. It is God who saves us from the fool's errand of self-justification and creates meaning for our lives. The attempt to define the nature and meaning of our existence as human beings is futile apart from our relationship to our creator. We were created in God's image to love and be loved, to be stewards on God's behalf: "The Lord God took the man and put him in the garden of Eden to till it and keep it" (Gen 2:15).

Stewards, yes, but even more. God declares our lives to have meaning and value by calling us to be partners—even "co-creators"—with God in making the world a more trustworthy, hopeful, and loving place! Luther taught that the unique being called human is placed between God and his neighbor as a means through which faith and love are received from above and distributed below in creation "just like a barrel or pipe, through which the spring of divine goodness ought to flow onto other people, without being impeded."[8] So, instead of doing deeds for God, God is active with us and in us as we till and keep the garden of creation. We are even partners with God in the task of reconciliation, namely, to bring about a right relationship between two parties. "In Christ God was reconciling the world to himself ... and entrusting the message of reconciliation to us" (2 Cor 5:19). And what a difference it makes to know that God's reconciliation will come to pass!

THE GOD WHO IS COMMUNITY AND EXTENDS COMMUNITY TO US

Finally, God speaks to a world where people struggle to establish meaningful connections with others. In the Word become flesh (John 1:14)—Jesus Christ—God promises belonging, not only with each other but as a part of a far bigger community. *Perichoresis* (Pare-ee-core-ay-sis) is a Greek word that means triune God and stresses the dynamic inter-relationship of the triune God as a divine community.[9] *Perichoresis* is the divine dance of the will of God (Father), the embodiment of God (Son), and the power of God (Holy Spirit). We will delve into this more deeply in Part II but for now, notice that God is depicted as plural in the book of Genesis: "Let *us* make humankind in *our* image, according to *our* likeness" (Gen 1:26).

God is community! Made in the image of God, we, too, are communal by nature, just as God is. The big takeaway is that God extends God's community to include us. As triune God, God has "emptied himself, taking the form of a servant" (Phil 2:7), and choosing to extend divine community to human beings in the dance of perichoresis. Often, community in the New Testament is described in even more intimate terms: as family. Here is how Paul addresses our estrangement: "So then you

---

8   Luther quoted in Bayer, *Luther's Theology*, 238n50.
9   Simpson, "Terrible Thing to Waste," 87-88.

are no longer strangers and aliens, but you are citizens with the saints and also members of the household of God." (Eph 2:19).

Henceforth, in this communal household, God puts on, or bears, our humanity and offers God's life to us. In the human community that has gathered at the cross, and by the power of the Holy Spirit, we, too, bear our neighbors' brokenness and confer the life of God to them. It is for this reason that Martin Luther crafted this gorgeous and profound quote: "We are Christ's—with and without the apostrophe."[10] This statement by Luther will be the basis of chapter 8. For now, note that it has a double meaning: having been included in God's triune community, we *belong* to Christ. Called to love our neighbor and help them bear their burdens, we are Christs to one another. How many times has a loving friend, neighbor, or family member picked us up and given us a hopeful sense of meaning by being there for us?

God gives us the gift of meaning, and it is sustenance for our souls. Through God's devoted presence within this world, the work to which we are called as partners with God, and the life-giving community that engenders meaningful relationships, we need not fall prey to the malaise of meaninglessness. And it all revolves around a God who seeks a relationship with us—a relationship in which we are called.

We are called

Missio Dei is a Latin phrase that means the mission of God. It encompasses all that God is up to in the world. We are invited to participate and share the missio Dei with God as participants in the perichoretic community. Indeed, we are called. We are the very means by which God carries out the missio Dei. We use the language of calling because it accurately depicts the personal relationship God has with us, as well as the urgency and importance of the task. God *calls* us. There are two questions to ask whenever we are not sure of our callings: *What is God up to in the world?* and *How are we a part of it?* Addressing these two questions together forms Christian community anytime, anywhere. And Christian community is always God-focused and participatory.

Our callings are also referred to as vocations, a word first used by Luther and the reformers to designate the work God calls us to do in our daily lives. How do we know what our callings are? Discernment. The practice

---

10 Luther quoted in Simpson, "Thinking with Luther," 371.

of learning how to identify God's call to us is discernment and it involves several considerations:

1. Since a calling comes out of a relationship with God, developing our relationship with God—both privately and corporately—is vital. This involves learning to listen to God and what God is up to so that one can better discern how and what God might be speaking to us.

2. Learning to listen to what our neighbors' needs are is a vital component of discernment.

3. Because we are finite creatures with a limited reach, we must learn to accept this limitation and know that we are not called to everything we can think of that is good. Rather, God calls us to do certain things because of *who* we are and *where* we are. Hence, discernment means sifting through the many possibilities to isolate where God is leaning. Therefore, part of discernment is learning to say *no* as well as yes.

4. A calling generally utilizes the gifts each of us has, hence, understanding our gifts is one important key to proper discernment.

Our gifts will largely—or at least, significantly—determine what our roles and callings will be. This book will focus on what our gifts are. We will find that these gifts are lenses to see more clearly how God is calling us. While we may think we don't have much to contribute to something as important as God's work, the truth is that you and I each have a treasure trove of gifts given to us by a loving God both as a personal blessing and for the sake of our neighbor. In fact, our gifts encompass much more than you might have thought, particularly from a Lutheran theological perspective. For instance, the daily places where you live your life are gifts, because that is where life and relationships unfold. Add to this such gifts as your personality, and your story—in all its joyful *and* painful moments.

We are already gifted with what we need to make a difference. The following gifts are capacities and opportunities for discerning how God is calling us, and we will examine them all more closely:

- Our places: God's Holy Spirit is at work in us in the places, relationships, and roles of our everyday lives.

- Our stories: Our stories intertwining with God's story can bless someone else's story.

- Our passions and values: God's Holy Spirit can partner with us by tapping into what motivates and guides us.

- Our personality: Our unique way of being in the world allows God to work in us in very particular ways.
- Our natural abilities: God utilizes what we're naturally good at to bless others.
- Gifts of the Spirit: God's Holy Spirit has harvested new gifts from the matrix of our personality, abilities, and life experience for the purpose of finding our unique role in building up the body of Christ and its witness in the world.

The combination of all these gifts constitutes a wonderful tapestry of uniqueness and giftedness that ensure everyone has a vital role to play in making the world a more trustworthy, loving, and hopeful place. The dynamics of forming a team according to each person's giftedness was delightfully illustrated in a memorable movie about rock music and a rogue teacher.

FILM CLIP

In the film, *School of Rock*, a substitute teacher hijacks a class in an exclusive private school to fulfill his objective of creating a rock band for a competition. While we don't condone his methods, the teacher effectively taps into the gifts of each student to create a band and support team where everyone's gifts are used. This is a lighthearted analogy that illustrates the idea that everyone has a place on the team. This is even more true of God's team, where everyone has not only one place but several places on the team.[11]

SUMMARY

In this chapter, we explored the modern existential crisis of meaninglessness that grows out of Western culture's displacement of God. As a result, we struggle with the pointlessness of our daily toil, the daunting challenge of creating our own meaning, and a much lonelier human existence. To these struggles we respond with good news! The God of scripture is very much present and at work in this fallen creation, calling each of us to partner with God in creating a more trustworthy, loving, and hopeful world. This is not only a world filled with meaning, it is a world where community is created and extended, just as the ragtag bunch of students found in *School of Rock*, where each one had a role to play on the team

---

11 Linklater, *School of Rock*.

as they learned to work together. What remains for each of us is the task of discerning—out of the many possible ways to spend our time—what God is calling us to do. We have wonderful clues to help us in this task, in the form of the many gifts God has showered us with, from our roles and relationships to our life story; from our unique personality to our natural abilities and spiritual gifts, etc.

In Chapter 2, we will examine gifts we all have in abundance: the places where we live our lives, the people who are there, and nature of the relationships that ensue. Indeed, it is where we spend most of our time in life. In Luther's theology, this was the primary arena for the priesthood of all believers and the place where we are called to obey God's Commandments and love our neighbor as ourselves.

Reflection and conversation: processing what you've learned

1. Does the description of the crisis of meaning and corresponding lack of hope seem right to you? Why or why not?

_____

_____

_____

2. Which of these is truer for you: The emptiness of the daily grind, the futility of creating your own meaning and worth, or the lack of authentic community? How about for your friends and neighbors?

_____

_____

_____

3. How might your daily life be different if God is there not primarily to judge but to love God's people and partner with them to do meaningful work?

_____

_____

_____

4. What are the ways that you experience meaning through community and belonging? Give examples.

_____

_____

_____

5. Do you find the whole idea of discerning what God is up to encouraging or daunting? Why?

_____

_____

_____

6. How does it affect your daily life and the practice of your faith to believe that meaning in life is grounded in our relationship with our creator who gives the gifts necessary for true meaning?

_____

_____

_____

Wrap-up

What takeaways do you have from Chapter 1?

_____

_____

_____

What questions do you have?

_____

_____

_____

God does not need our works,
but our neighbor does.

—*Gustaf Wingren, Luther on Vocation*

CHAPTER 2

THE GIFT OF YOUR PLACES IN LIFE

Review and reflection

In Chapter 1, we began with the crisis of meaning in our culture—a crisis largely created by a rapidly developing culture that has pronounced God either dead, distant, or disposable. None of these cultural perceptions make it so, however. On the contrary, I am asserting that the God of Christianity has not been pushed aside but is present, committed to this world, and is ever engaged in creating anew a more trustworthy, loving, and hopeful world! What truly gives our daily existence meaning and hope is that we are called to join God in that task—each of us, along with countless others in a community God has extended to us. And this calling starts right in front of our noses, as we shall soon see.

What resonated with you from Chapter 1 as we discussed the plight of meaninglessness and God's response?

_____

_____

_____

What would you like to explore more?

_____

_____

_____

CHAPTER OVERVIEW

Contrary to the popular wisdom of his time, Luther taught that we are called to partner with God in the world right where we live our lives every day and with the people to whom we relate. As we shall see, this is not the place where folks in Luther's day expected God to be at work, and they certainly didn't understand that their daily grind had anything to do with callings from God! But Luther's teaching means that for us, changing diapers, selling widgets at a fair price, and attending caucuses are somehow part of God's mission! In fact, these everyday places where we live our lives, and carry out our roles as parents, spouses, coworkers, neighbors, and citizens are callings of the *highest* order. God is at work in and through our mundane efforts, creating with us a more trustworthy world. The places where we live our lives and form our relationships—the *terra firma* of life—are indeed profound gifts to us, even in our often compromised life conditions. But these gifts of place are also meant by God to be gifts for our neighbor, occasions for loving them and pursuing the common good together with our neighbor. In this chapter, we will examine the places where we live our lives and what our callings look like there. These places and roles account for the most significant and extensive callings we have in this world. After all, this is where we spend most of our lives.

Introduction to the gift of your places in life

FILM CLIP

In the movie, *Nobody's Fool*, Sully (played by Paul Newman) is a charming but selfish person, accountable to no one. This leads to estrangement from his ex-wife, his son and grandson, and—we will soon discover—his friend who badly needs encouragement. Through the daily ebb and flow of this small New England town, Sully gains the affection of a lonely and beautiful younger woman who eventually wants to run off with him to Hawaii. It seems like a slam-dunk move for someone so untethered to other's needs and expectations. Yet at the moment of truth, Sully realizes he can't go with her. He has a breakthrough as he reflects on place, roles, and relationships. He rediscovers and re-engages three callings right in front of him of which he was only dimly aware before, namely, to his son, grandson, and friend. They all need Sully to be a life-giving presence in their lives. What callings can be found in our primary places, roles, and relationships?[1]

LEARNING: SURELY GOD IS IN THIS PLACE

In Genesis 28:10–17, we learn that Jacob discovered God in the last place he expected to find God: in the middle of the wilderness with someone like himself. Since Jacob had just stolen his older brother's birthright and was now fleeing from his wrath, it could reasonably be surmised that Jacob was running from God, too. Suffice it to say, in his lonely place of hiding in the wilderness—a place often assumed to be the haunt of demons—Jacob probably did not expect God to show up unless it was to strike him down. But that is not what God did. God had good news for Jacob, blessing him right there under the stars *in order to* be a blessing to all the families of the earth.

Is God also in places you don't expect, working to bless you and, through you, bless others? The fact that you, like Jacob, are compromised in this life does not disqualify you. God is used to working through a flawed medium and with flawed people. Particularly when they know they are flawed!

Surely God is *not* in this place: The world of Luther's time

In Martin Luther's time, Roman Catholicism held some fairly contradictory positions regarding the secular world. While the world was considered sacred by virtue of being God's creation, it was also considered profane and *fallen*, reflecting the sinful distortions that human beings and the work of the devil had wrought within it. In many ways, the secular world where human beings lived and worked was thought to be a lost cause. This had two huge implications. First of all, the world of Luther's time was not considered humanity's true home.[2] Our home and destiny were elsewhere,

---

1 Benton, *Nobody's Fool*, 1:30:54–1:34:17.
2 This insight is shared courtesy of a conversation with Dr. Mark Tranvik, professor of church history at Luther Seminary.

namely, in heaven. The world, then, being seen as a temporary layover of sorts, the created world and its activity became devalued, fostering the sense that God was not actively at work in it or its residents.

Second, for a church member to secure a spot in their true home—heaven—Catholics believed that human beings needed to become acceptable to God by climbing a spiritual ladder that transcended the messed-up world in which they lived. Only by becoming righteous—like Christ—could they go to heaven. Since they couldn't become righteous on their own, God bestowed grace to those who had faith and took the sacraments. But then it was the job of the believer to use the grace given to them, do good deeds, and ascend a spiritual ladder of progress. If one utilized their grace in this way, then God would give them more grace. However, if you didn't use the grace and accumulate enough merit, God may not gift you with any more grace. The truth is, it was hard to accumulate enough merit in a profane world that lacked sufficient holiness. So, many people ended up in purgatory waiting for a relative with enough merit (or money) to spring them loose into heaven. With few good options for advancement, it was easy to despair of one's lot.

How could you accumulate enough merit? By having a legitimate Christian calling and devoting your life to extraordinary pursuits that were sacred, of a godly nature—in other words, the institutional church. The only people who had callings, then, were those in the Roman Catholic Church: priests, monks, nuns, cardinals, bishops, and so on. To get closer to God, many men would leave their families back in the foul world to pursue the priesthood or enter a monastery. Women would forgo becoming mothers to become nuns instead. Needless to say, there were many, many monasteries and convents full of people who had left one world (the profane and ordinary) to enter another one (the sacred and extraordinary). Martin Luther had a lot to say about this sociological phenomenon.

Luther and the God who wears masks

But as we learned in Chapter 1, God is no stranger to this world. In the world according to Luther—and scripture—a different conclusion than that of the prevailing Catholicism is reached: surely God *is* in this place! Indeed, the secular world that is often profane is in fact sacred ground not only because God made it and loves it, but because what transpires in human history matters. Luther held that the everyday, ordinary world we inhabit for business, commerce, education, public life, government, and family life—the "orders" of creation—is God's world and God is at work there, albeit hidden behind "masks."[3] Masks here are simply the people, functions, and orders themselves. Furthermore, while we have the promise of a resurrected life in heaven, this promise is to be viewed less as a rejection of this world and more as a fulfillment of the life and history of this world. God's work—and ours—is to create a trustworthy world where life can thrive. None of this means the world is pure, untainted, and without profanity. Far from it. It simply means God is there and God values what and who is there. The division between sacred and secular is wrong. God is as much at work in the world as in the church. This idea predates the reformers, though. As a church historian notes, "Early Christians thought not of going to church but church being present at their employment."[4] It means that callings are anytime, anywhere: at work, at play, at home.

And this raises the question, again, about our true home. Drawing heavily on scripture, Luther develops the position that the *true home* of the human being is not a place at all, but a relationship. To love and trust God is to live in a restored relationship that represents our truest nature as human beings. We are not called to rise above our earthly constraints as creatures in some ethereal, spiritual sense. Rather, we are called to embrace our creaturehood as beings who are *dependent* on God who alone is transcendent! Our spirituality, if you will, embraces our whole—and material—self while being in a relationship with the transcendent God. So, it doesn't matter where we are, but *with whom* we are, and what sort of relationship that is. This is what it means to be fully human: to live within the community of creation while rooted in faith in a loving, sustaining, and ever-creating God! That is our home, plain and simple.

The world is sacred to Luther because of what it says in John 1:3, "All things were made through him (Christ)." This means that Luther is panentheistic, which means, *all (pan)-in (en)-God (theist)*, or, God is in all. As one theologian has written, while expressing Lutheran theology brilliantly, "Either God is *in* matter or God *doesn't* matter."[5] The message is clear: for God to make a difference in human existence, God must be present and deeply invested in God's creation! The trees, the mountains, and the wolves all pulsate with the presence of God who is at the same time beyond the material universe. Wearing the masks of this world, God is present and active in all persons, including scientists, teachers, and hotel maids, as well as those playing at a park and selling in a marketplace. God is present in activities and institutions that work to protect and foster life,

---

3 Westhelle, *Transfiguring*, 144-54.
4 Schuurman, *Discerning our Callings*, 35-36.
5 Westhelle, , 160.

animating the best impulses of a university, legislature, or corporation. It is important to add, however, that while God is in all things and all of creation, God also stands apart from it and is transcendent. Neither can it be assumed that God's activity within people and institutions is always an endorsement! Clearly, a God of love and justice is often at odds with the flawed partners of this world!

It should come as no surprise then that the very work of people in the everyday, nonchurch world suddenly takes on new significance, as God is already at work there, calling us to be willing partners with God in co-creating a more trustworthy, loving, and hopeful world. As I noted in the preface, Luther introduced us to the idea of the priesthood of all believers. By this, Luther means that the work lay people do in their lives, the places—or stations—they occupy and the roles they fill as parents and children, are callings from God. Consequently, Luther dared suggest that the callings of mother and father, farmer and lawyer, merchant and citizen are as important and godly as that of priest or monk. It is there—in the everyday world—that we meet God who is already at work. In fact, there is no higher calling than being a parent (including any calling in the church). Hence, according to Luther, a father changing a diaper was God's work and calling![6]

But just below parenting, skilled and unskilled employment, as well as civic participation also constitute holy ground for Luther. As priests, monks, and bishops were thought to be the only real callings/vocations, Luther stands this notion on its head when he declares, "There is no true, basic difference between laymen and priests, princes and bishops, between the religious and the secular, except for the sake of office and work, but not for the sake of status. They are all of the same spiritual estate and are all truly priests, bishops, and popes. But they do not all have the same work to do."[7]

So, the next time someone asks, "Who made you Pope?" just say, "Martin Luther did. Or at least he made me bishop."

SAVED *FROM* THE WORLD OR SAVED *FOR* THE WORLD?

In Luther's time, it was widely held that we were saved from the world, and the way to do that was by ascending to positions and practices that were away from—or above—the world. Because salvation was in doubt

---

6 Wengert, *Catechisms*, 151-55.
7 Luther quoted in Gritsch and Jenson, *Lutheranism*, 111.

until someone attained the proper righteousness or spiritual elevation, the earnest Christian was consumed with doing things that would elevate him/herself. Any good deeds done in the world were done for advancement, not necessarily out of love. This only further devalued the world as a means to an end rather than an end in itself.

For instance, in Luther's time, there was a movement of laypeople who wanted to eradicate poverty in Rome. "Why just give alms to the poor when we have a chance to address the roots of poverty and erase it?" they asked. The pope ruled on this movement and its goals, and the ruling was not favorable. The pope argued that if poverty were eliminated, so too would many opportunities for people to do good deeds for the poor. Hence, the pope rejected the idea.[8] Whose interests are being served here? Again, the world is seen here not as something to be valued and stewarded but as a means for my own ticket off the planet.

Luther argued that we are saved not *from* the world but *for* the world. Since salvation is a free gift of justification received in faith, no ladder climbing is necessary. The result is that in our freedom, we can focus on loving our neighbor without worrying about our status before God, which has been taken care of. We can go back into our world and love our neighbor for our neighbor's sake, not our own advancement. In fact, we must! Tellingly, the ancient Greek word for church—*Ekklesia*—means "a people called out of the world in order to serve God in the world."[9] The church fathers were pretty clear that the business of the church is immersion in the world—God's world—not escape or isolation.

The Ten Commandments and the call to love

As Luther made clear numerous times, faith not only can produce good works, it must! When we are justified by God's grace through faith, we are restored to who we were created to be: loving members of the community of creation. And how do we love all the people denoted by the designation "neighbor"—our neighbors and strangers, coworkers and family members? By observing the Ten Commandments. As Jesus said, the law can be summed up in two simple commands: love God and love neighbor. The arenas where we live our lives, namely, the real world, is precisely where we carry out the commands God gave us to love. What is critical to understand—and Luther understood this well—is that the Commandments are far more than prohibitions (don't do this, don't do that). In the spirit of love, the Commandments invite *proactive* behavior on our part. So,

---

8 Haemig, lecture.
9 Schuurman, *Callings*, 17-18.

as Luther pointed out, we are not merely to refrain from doing harm to our neighbor, but also proactively do whatever we can to help our neighbor's life thrive and be whole! For instance, in Luther's *Small Catechism*, he interprets the meaning of the fifth commandment that "you shall not murder" (Exod 20:13) as follows: "We are to fear and love God, so that we neither endanger nor harm the lives of our neighbors, but instead help them and support them in all of life's needs."[10] Think of how much this clarification changes what it means to be a "good" Christian. A whole lot more than just keeping out of trouble, that's for sure!

There is another thing worth noting on the subject of love that is critical, about its very definition. The contemporary definition of love is quite different from the New Testament notion of *agape* love. It is almost universally the case in modern culture that when one refers to love, they mean an emotion or feeling they have toward someone—though not necessarily a romantic feeling. This feeling may or may not be accompanied by any sense of commitment. When this is the case, the capacity to do the right thing for the sake of the person you love is contingent on the feelings of love that bind you to that person. *Agape* love, as explicated in the Pauline writings, for instance, is not rooted in feeling and emotion, though feeling and emotion may accompany this kind of love. Rather, *agape* love is a commitment, rooted in speech and action that always seeks the well-being of the beloved. Whether or not emotion or feeling is present is peripheral, for the command to love our neighbor is not predicated on liking them or having feelings of love toward them, as that is not something one can control, anyway. Rather, *agape* love is simply a perspective, a commitment of one's will to speak and act in such a way that serves the interests of my neighbor. As we will find out more in Part II, this kind of love, pure and unmotivated, comes to us from beyond as a gift. We receive it in partnership with God who is at work with and in us.

How can—and how does—God work through you at the places where you live your life, coaxing you to love as a commitment? It may not seem like your everyday, mundane life in the secular world constitutes a calling and opportunity to do meaningful work in partnership with God, but indeed it does! Nothing illustrates how much a calling can do to restore one's sense of being alive than a famous film from post-war Japan.

---

10 Luther, *Small Catechism*, 16.

FILM CLIP

One of Akira Kurosawa's greatest movies is about a Tokyo man in the 1950s who discovers he has terminal cancer and realizes he's never really lived in the first place. The movie is entitled, *Ikiru*, and it shows us the life of Kanji, a city manager who is part of a bureaucracy that is notorious for pushing paper, but not responding to actual needs. As Kanji takes time off from work to deal with his illness, he is drawn to a young woman whose company he seeks not for romantic reasons, but because she is full of life. He discovers that she does things to make others' lives better. Soon he has a lightbulb experience. He will henceforth be committed to serving the common good in his city manager position. From that point on, he is relentless with his fellow bureaucrats and superiors to see that a park gets built to replace a sewage-infested vacant lot that endangers the well-being of the children in that neighborhood. He dies a happy man because the park is built and it gives life to the neighborhood and its children, all because he decided to use his station in life—his everyday job—to bring life to others.[11]

SUMMARY

As we can see in Kurosawa's great movie, *Ikiru*, the opportunities to make the world more trustworthy and life-giving are right in front of us. While many consider religion as an escape from the material world to our true spiritual home, Christian faith asserts that the material world where we live is not only created by God but inhabited by God, who is constantly at work. In other words (but in no way disputing the promise of heaven that awaits us), we're not saved *from* the world, but *for* the world! And this God who is loose in the world calls us daily to first of all celebrate the gifts we have been given in the form of the people, places, and activities that make up our lives. Second, we are called forth where we live, work, and play to join God in the work of co-creating a more trustworthy and hopeful world. This co-creating is best summarized by the Commandments, which quite simply call for us to love our neighbor as ourselves. It is imperative, then, that we reflect on how God is at work with and through us in our work, our roles, and our relationships.

In the next chapter, we will consider how it is that from the matrix of places, people, relationships, and events that make up our lives, there

---

11 Kurosawa, *Ikiru*.

emerges for all of us a story that is our own. And that story is where God meets broken human beings, transforming our story into a gift for us and for those around us. We will unpack the gift of your story in chapter 3.

Reflection and conversation: processing what you've learned

1. Make a list of the primary places where you live your life: home, work, and play.

_____

_____

_____

2. Now identify the primary roles/relationships you have at those places and list them: parent, spouse, practitioner, friend, citizen, church member, etc.

_____

_____

_____

3. How are these places, relationships, and roles a gift to you? How are you blessed by them? (Before we entertain how they are a gift to others, it's important to perceive God's rich bounty of gifts for my own benefit as well.)

_____

_____

_____

4. How are your places a gift to others? What is God up to at your places?

_____

_____

_____

5. What are your callings at each of your primary places? (If you list to "be a good dad," in what way?) Write out each of your calls (corresponding to each of your places/roles) in one sentence so they have some focus and particularity.

_____

_____

_____

6. Which callings (from your primary places/roles) give you the most satisfaction? Why?

_____

_____

_____

7. In which places/roles is it the most difficult to imagine God being active?

_____

_____

_____

8. How do you feel about love as primarily commitment (sometimes accompanied by feelings), rather than feelings (that may or may not involve any commitment) toward someone?

_____

_____

_____

9. Which commandments are most important to your callings in daily life? Write down some of your callings next to the most relevant commandments. (For example, if you are an accountant, you might consider not bearing false witness a key commandment.) Remember the proactive meanings of the commandments, courtesy of Luther!

a. The first commandment: You shall have no other gods. Rather, you shall love the Lord your God with all your heart, mind, and soul.

_____

_____

b. The second commandment: You shall not take the name of the Lord, your God, in vain. Rather, you shall use God's name in praise, thanksgiving, and direct address for all of life's needs.

_____

_____

c. The third commandment: You shall keep the day of rest holy.

_____

_____

d. The fourth commandment: Honor your father and your mother, that it may be well with you, and that you may live long on the earth.

_____

_____

e. The fifth commandment: You shall not kill. Rather, you shall seek and support the health and well-being of your neighbor.

_____

_____

f. The sixth commandment: You shall not commit adultery. Rather, you shall respect other people as whole persons whose bodies are temples of God.

_____

_____

g. The seventh commandment: You shall not steal. Rather, you shall help your neighbor protect what is theirs.

_____

_____

h. The eighth commandment: You shall not bear false witness against your neighbor. Rather, you shall defend, speak well of, and put the most charitable interpretation possible on your neighbor's actions.

_____

_____

i. The ninth commandment: You shall not covet your neighbor's house. Rather, you shall help your neighbor protect what is hers or his, and seek to be free from desire for things.

_____

_____

j. The tenth commandment: You shall not covet your neighbor's wife, nor his manservant, nor his maidservant, nor his cattle, nor anything that is his. Rather, you shall help your neighbor's family and workers be loyal to your neighbor.

_____

_____

Wrap-up

What questions do you have about Chapter 2?

_____

_____

_____

What takeaways do you have?

_____

_____

_____

When we become aware that we do not have
to escape our pains, but that we can mobilize
them into a common search for life, those very
pains are transformed from expressions of
despair into signs of hope.

—*Henri Nouwen, The Wounded Healer*

CHAPTER 3

THE GIFT OF YOUR STORY

Review and reflection

In the first two chapters, we've offered a counter-narrative to the existential query, What's the point of it all? In a world not only created by God but filled with God's presence and activity, there is aim and purpose. Furthermore, when each of us are invited to partner with God for the purpose of protecting life and helping it thrive and flourish, now you have a world worth living in! And, as we discovered in the previous chapter, meaningful work for each of us is precisely within the contours of our everyday existence—at the places we live and work, with the people who are in our lives, through the roles we take on in all those circumstances. These easily overlooked gifts of place and people ground our lives just as they are opportunities to love our neighbor.

What is resonating from Chapter 2 as we discussed your places in life?

_____

_____

_____

What loose ends or questions do you have from Chapter 2?

_____

_____

_____

CHAPTER OVERVIEW

There is a powerful gift that emerges from the ebb and flow of a person's daily life. At the places we live, with the people who are there, in the roles we play, and within the events that transpire in our lives, a story is being told—a narrative that is your story. Our stories come with suffering, doubts, and questions, where we may wonder at times why God didn't seem to show up in our lives when we needed God. But our stories also come with overcoming and with hope, joy, and beauty.

And, of course, one's own story inevitably raises the question of meaning or meaninglessness, namely, Is God's hand evident in my story or is my life just a series of random responses to various events? So, _does_ God have a plan for your life? What if you miss the plan and get it wrong? Scripture and life itself bear witness to the fact that the script for our story is in constant revision. In this chapter, we will explore a particular promise from God: No matter what has transpired in our lives, no matter how many mistakes we may have made and doubts that have plagued us, we are joined and uplifted in our struggle. Ultimately, our story—with all of its light and darkness—is a gift because it is intertwined with God's story in an act of solidarity, love, and redemption. Whether we always perceive this or not, we are promised that God's story is at work in and through our story, filling our story with meaning. This is a theology of the cross, and it takes seriously God's suffering and ours, all for the sake of hope and rebirth.

And so it is that we can bear witness to our own God-infused story as a source of promise, solidarity, and hope to those around us. The gift of your story is that it is uniquely yours, but never isolated. Because our stories are weaved together with God's story, they are also interwoven with the stories of many others in the community of God, creating a new narrative for you that is undergirded by grace, hope, and calling. Indeed, our stories have uniquely prepared us for certain callings born right out of our own life experiences. Regardless of how difficult your story may or may not be, you are a witness to a broken life redeemed, and therefore, a potential advocate for someone else.

Introduction to the gift of your story

Sometimes we think personal weakness or shortcoming is nothing but a liability. In one unique film, the central character wrestles with what he believes is a special purpose that he is destined for. What that is, he doesn't know, but upon discovering what it is, he never would have imagined it would be on account of one very significant shortcoming of his.

> **FILM CLIP**
>
> In the movie, *Simon Birch*, Simon is a boy with severely stunted growth who is also a restless, searching soul. He struggles to find his place in his adolescent world and openly shares with anyone who will listen that God has a plan for his life. He just doesn't know what it is. While he absorbs the skeptical reactions from most of the adults in his life—including, sadly, his pastor—he waits until the unfolding of his life makes it clear how his identity and story have uniquely prepared him for a very important purpose.[1] This example of wondering and waiting for clarity is a powerful reflection on the ambiguity of life while also embracing faith in the midst of it.

LEARNING: GOD'S STORY AND MINE

Theologies of God's plan for my life

As we wrestle with how our own story is an instrument for God's purposes, it may become confusing for us. We are well aware of the imperfections and flaws of our story, and the times—sometimes lengthy—when we were adrift or felt God wasn't there for us. The following are some theological options available in popular culture for coming to understand how God might be at work in our lives.

---

1 Johnson,

THE MASTER PLAN

Many people—Christian teachers and leaders included—believe that God has a *master plan* for your life. It's all laid out in advance and constitutes God's will for you. But if God does have a master plan for your life, what are the chances you both correctly perceive it and follow the plan obediently? These are of course rhetorical questions. Considering all the ways we struggle and stumble in life, it seems like a foregone conclusion we'll wander astray at some point from whatever God's plan is for us. So, how do you redeem your life if you choose the wrong plan and are on the wrong path? With all the bad decisions we make and all the times we fail to discern God's will, if there's a master plan, it's a pretty good bet we missed it! Then what?

EVERYTHING HAPPENS FOR A REASON

How often do we hear people say this in response to whatever happens in life? No matter what event or circumstances occur, one might be comforted by the assurance from someone that everything happens for a reason, presumably foreordained by God. No danger of missing God's plan here! Whatever happened was planned by God in the first place. It's predetermined and therefore a form of philosophical *determinism*, which raises serious problems. First of all, if the bad things that happen to us are caused by God, does that make God responsible for evil? Second, if the things that happen to us—and the life decisions we make—are predetermined, then whatever happened to our free will? If we're just puppets in a cosmic puppet show, we have lost agency and are no longer a partner or co-creator with God in this world. Determinism leaves us in a pretty meaningless state of affairs.

PROCESS THEOLOGY

What if God works in real-time with the stuff of our compromised lives that define our stories, always pointing to new and possible outcomes? Simply put, it may be the case that God is in *process* with us, joining us on our life's journey in real-time and helping us navigate a way forward. In this case, God's story intertwines with ours as we live into the future, step by step. This theology reflects much of scripture where God is in a dynamic relationship with God's people (and us), constantly working with them to redeem their broken world. However, unlike the scriptural narrative, process theology depicts a smaller God that does not transcend time but is in real-time with us. Furthermore, the biblical God is in control of human history's outcome through re-creation and establishing the kingdom of God. Process theology, on the other hand, strongly suggests that human history—and therefore, God—is at the mercy of what humans decide. I can already feel my hope waning.

Theology of the cross: the God who died redeems our story

For Lutherans and many other Christians, the best way to answer how our flawed journeys through life can be a gift to anyone is best understood by cultivating a theology of the cross. This theology asserts that the cross—the cross symbolizing the entire life, suffering, and death of Jesus—tells us what we need to know about how God is present and at work in our lives. What does the cross tell us about God? That God shows up most profoundly in human lives when things are the worst; when our story has become sad, even tragic. God's willingness to endure persecution, torture, abandonment, and even death tells us that God's loving purpose was (and is) to experience and share in the very worst of human experience. Why? To once and for all defeat the powers that put God on the cross (and which threaten to destroy our own narratives as well) in order to be raised to new life. Not just for God's own sake, of course, but for ours. A theology of the cross is about redemption. No matter what life throws at us—including the consequences of our own decisions—God can and does bring life out of the mess, thereby redeeming our broken existence. More than that, God even finds value in the broken stuff of life, using these narrative shards as elements for a new narrative of death and rebirth!

One of the implications of a theology of the cross is that we can view our life story differently. Instead of pretending that being a Christian has made life a bed of roses for you, you can be honest and call a spade a spade. God meets you right where you struggle and question, and without erasing the struggle, has taken up your story into God's own story through Jesus Christ! After all, what greater cry of solidarity could Jesus have ever uttered than his forlorn prayer/protest: "My God, my God, why have you forsaken me?" (Matt 27:46). Truth be told, a theology of the cross describes our lives better than resurrection does. Faith or not, this life is often marked by pain, doubt, and brokenness. In our current existence, we know and confess that we are in bondage to sin, even as we are heartened by the good news that is our hope and promise. The cross is where we live and must live in order to die, that we might rise! That means our own stories must be told honestly with the faith that God is in the midst of my story working for salvation.

What does the theology of the cross and process theology mean for our life stories and our understanding of callings? However rough around the edges and compromised our life stories are, in the hands of the God who died on the cross and rose again, our lives are transformed in God's unfolding story. Our story (even the difficult parts) is a gift because our story is exactly where God has promised to show up, weaving God's story with ours in an act of solidarity, love, and redemption. Romans 8:28 says this: "We know that all things work together for good for those who love God, who are called according to his purpose." What does it mean? It means that whatever happens in life—even if it is produced by profound brokenness and sin—is fertile soil for new growth, even resurrection. This verse does not say that all things *are* good. They clearly are not, nor does God will all things. It does say that all things *work for the good* for those God has called according to his purpose. God can bring life even out of death, and force bad seeds to produce good fruit.

As we are Christs to our neighbor, that same broken story of ours can be a proclamation to someone else that God is with them in their pain, bears that pain with them, and promises resurrection and wholeness to us. My own story includes the experience of losing my younger brother David when he was only twenty-five years old. While it was hard for me, it was harder for my parents, I think. How does a parent deal with such deep despair? My mom and dad coauthored a book where they told their story of faith and grief.[2] Titled *The Five Cries of Grief*, their book has gone through five printings so far. Why is it so popular? Because two broken parents wrote about what shook them to the core and where they saw God in all of it. That is something that resonates for virtually anyone who has gone through this experience. My parents dared to believe that their tragic experience was also a calling. And that calling was, and is, to use your experience as an opportunity to bear witness to a God who brings life out of the worst things life can throw at us.

What my parents experienced with this is similar to how many movements start. There is immense pain followed by a resolve to turn that pain into a declaration of solidarity with others in pain. This is the community Christ gathers at the cross: broken people being brought together out of the pain of life's crucible—whether one's own or their neighbor's. And so, a theology of the cross reveals a *cruciform* community gathered at the foot of the cross, living out the shape of God's ongoing mission to us and with us: to seek the marginalized and those in need of a physician to bring good news and the community of God to them. A theology of the cross

---

2 Strommen, *Five Cries.*

gains much of its power because it takes place on the journey of life, a road we recognize well where stories are being formed. A road that is hopeful because it is based on the story of the God who is in solidarity with us—in death and resurrection.

JOURNEY THEOLOGY: A THEOLOGY ON THE ROAD

People often view the Bible in legal terms, i.e., as a constitution with inviolable laws. If you want to find out what you're supposed to do or not do, look it up in the Bible. It's the book with all the answers, at least according to popular understanding. Some have suggested that the Bible is an acronym standing for Basic Instructions Before Leaving Earth. I've also heard the Bible referred to as the users' manual for life.

These understandings are not helpful because they assume the following attitude: *Just tell me what to do, God, and I'll do it.* But if "good religion" is reduced to getting the right instructions or laws, then who needs God? We humans like to be in control and have a habit of not needing God. There's a word for that: sin. We create deep ditches for ourselves when we think the law or the right instructions are our salvation, because then our lives are about us, not God. A theology of the cross reminds us in no uncertain terms who we human beings are: To put it bluntly, we killed God, and Jesus's death is also the death of our pretensions and ways. No, a theology of the cross does not allow us to distance ourselves from the Romans and Jewish leaders who sentenced Jesus to death. Instead, they are a microcosm of what sin looks like in the sweep of human history—an often-merciless history that includes all of us and lives in all of us. And so, we who are in the grips of unfaith must die to rise again. Through faith, God will give us new life.

No, the Bible is not a constitution or instruction manual, it is a story—the story of God's faithfulness in the face of unrelenting human folly. To be sure, laws and commandments are *a part of* the story. They serve the story and were given by God as an act of love to restrain sin, prompt obedience, and remind us of our folly. But laws always focus on what God expects of us—expectations that are largely unfulfilled in our fallen state. The unfolding story we find in the Bible is all about what God does for us in an ongoing drama of sin and redemption, death and resurrection, rebellion and coming home again. When we think in terms of the rhythms of a story—not a constitution or book of instructions—then we are closer to the pulse of God and where God meets us. God breaks into our own winding story and in the process creates a new story of solidarity, hope, and promise. On this journey, God is present with us through the Holy Spirit and God's Son, calling us forward into life even amid painful passages. A journey theology takes place on the road of life and it means learning to identify how you are blessed—again, even with the presence of suffering—and how you in turn can be a blessing. Such a story as yours can offer a point of common understanding, solidarity, and ultimately hopefulness that God is present in their story as well.

It must be noted, also, that learning to identify and weave stories together—God's and ours—is not easy work. This is a great example of what it means to "do theology," namely, to reflect and work through our understanding of how God is present in our lives—past, present, and future. Understanding the Bible as a story requires ongoing and dynamic conversation in which we participate with the living God, and where we are not always asking the questions! God has a few questions of his own for us to reflect on as we journey. And, of course, we have questions about our own stories because much of the time, we are not clear what our own story means or where it's going. A theology of the cross (which is a very particular journey theology) encourages questions because it assumes living life in a broken world where clarity is often missing.

Questions, conversation, interpreting our stories. The whole activity of weaving our stories with God's ought not to be a solitary exercise between just me and God. Here is where we humans on the road are called to let our respective narratives be gifts to one another. If God is asking questions of us and we are wrestling with our own stories, we need each other to help us reflect and make sense of it all. For this reason, Luther described "the mutual conversation and consolation of the saints"[3] as an essential element in Christian life, almost declaring it a new sacrament. When Christians gather in the name of (and with Jesus) to tell their stories, reflect on God's presence and leading in those stories, find support from one another in darker passages, and listen together for where God is calling them, this is mutual conversation and consolation. It may be in a group of ten or two, but it is a powerful way of receiving blessings from God through others and blessing others by being there for them.

Nowhere in scripture do the themes of journey, conversation, and divine purpose show up more clearly than in Luke's account of the road to Emmaus. Here, a three-way conversation illustrates beautifully doing theology on the road, and even more specifically, *theologia crucis*.

---

3 Luther quoted in Linman, "Mutual Conversation," 1.

WHEN GOD'S STORY MEETS OURS ON THE ROAD TO EMMAUS
Read Luke 24:13-35.

Now on that same day, two of them were going to a village called Emmaus, about seven miles from Jerusalem, and talking with each other about all these things that had happened. While they were talking and discussing, Jesus himself came near and went with them, but their eyes were kept from recognizing him. And he said to them, 'What are you discussing with each other while you walk along?' They stood still, looking sad. Then one of them, whose name was Cleopas, answered him, 'Are you the only stranger in Jerusalem who does not know the things that have taken place there in these days?' He asked them, 'What things?' They replied, 'The things about Jesus of Nazareth, who was a prophet mighty in deed and word before God and all the people, and how our chief priests and leaders handed him over to be condemned to death and crucified him. But we had hoped that he was the one to redeem Israel. Yes, and besides all this, it is now the third day since these things took place. Moreover, some women in our group astounded us. They were at the tomb early this morning, and when they did not find his body there, they came back and told us that they had indeed seen a vision of angels who said that he was alive. Some of those who were with us went to the tomb and found it just as the women had said; but they did not see him.' Then he said to them, 'Oh, how foolish you are, and how slow of heart to believe all that the prophets have declared! Was it not necessary that the Messiah should suffer these things and then enter into his glory?' Then beginning with Moses and all the prophets, he interpreted to them the things about himself in all the scriptures.

As they came near the village to which they were going, he walked ahead as if he were going on. But they urged him strongly, saying, 'Stay with us, because it is almost evening and the day is now nearly over.' So, he went in to stay with them. When he was at the table with them, he took bread, blessed and broke it, and gave it to them. Then their eyes were opened, and they recognized him, and he vanished from their sight. They said to each other, 'Were not our hearts burning within us while he was talking to us on the road, while he was opening the scriptures to us?' That same hour they got up and returned to Jerusalem, and they found the eleven and their companions gathered together. They were saying, 'The Lord has risen indeed, and he has appeared to Simon!' Then they told what had happened on the road, and how he had been made known to them in the breaking of the bread.

Reflection and conversation on the road to Emmaus

1. Let's collect what we know about the stories of Cleopas and the other disciple of Jesus. As they walked on that road to Emmaus, what were their recent and present stories?

_____

_____

_____

2. Have you ever been in a similar situation of despair and hopelessness?

_____

_____

_____

3. What helped you move through it?

_____

_____

_____

4. What is the importance of their conversation with the stranger on the road to Emmaus?

_____

_____

_____

5. How does God's story—embodied in Jesus—impact Cleopas and his friend's stories?

_____

_____

_____

6. When did they understand that Jesus was with them?

_____

_____

_____

Often, it's after the fact that we understand the significance of our story. Notice that it was through conversation that they processed what happened. In reflection, they observed, "Were not our hearts burning within us?"

7. When have you looked back on your life and realized there was more going on than you were aware of at the time?

_____

_____

_____

8. What was the result of their story merging with Jesus' story? Your story can play a role in a much larger story.

_____

_____

_____

SUMMARY

Out of the ebb and flow of daily existence, your life's narrative is formed and it's a gift to you because it is uniquely yours, you are not traveling alone, and it is filled with hope and promise. Unlike the theologies that peddle a notion of God's plan for your life that is completely scripted, we do not experience life that way. It is unpredictable, we make mistakes, and we are improvising a lot. And yet God is there no matter what, to help us bear life's burden, make sense of it all, and point the way to life. No matter how much pain and doubt may have accompanied the joyful and satisfying elements of your story, all of it is a gift because it is right there in the real stuff of life where God meets us in solidarity through Christ, weaving together our story with God's. Like Cleopas and his friend on the road to Emmaus, our lives are filled with grief and questions, and yet there is another story, another person who joins us on the road. And this other story transforms our own, redeeming our suffering, confirming our joy, and pointing us to love our neighbor with what we've learned on the road. Our story is a gift to us and our neighbor because it tells another story: our stories are taken up by God as God's own story, sharing in our suffering while promising new life. And it is a profound gift that we can share our stories and help one another understand their own.

In chapter 4, we will explore two features of one's life that are indispensable for a life well lived. The first one is values and the second one is passions. As we shall see, values help give a life story guard rails for its direction and substance, while passions help give a person the energy and fuel to get things done. Values and passions, when they are in alignment with love, are immeasurable gifts to the subject and to their neighbor.

Reflection and conversation on the gift of your story

1. Write your life story as a one-page (or less) novel. What are the key developments and key people involved? How does your character change or develop over time?

Or, if you prefer, identify your life as chapter titles. What would the chapters be, and what titles would you use for each chapter?

_____

_____

_____

2. How is your story unique? What are the experiences that make your story you? Boil the story down to one word or phrase.

_____

_____

_____

3. How is your story a gift to you? Where are the blessings?

_____

_____

_____

4. When has God shown up in your story to bless it? When did you feel God was absent?

_____

_____

_____

5. How could the suffering and doubt you experience in life be a gift to others?

_____

_____

_____

6. What are unique parts of your story that could encourage or help others?

_____

_____

_____

7. What is God calling you to do and be because of your story?

_____

_____

_____

Wrap-up

What questions do you have about Chapter 3?

_____

_____

_____

What takeaways do you have?

_____

_____

_____

The place God calls you to is the place where your deep gladness and the world's deep hunger meet.

—*Frederick Buechner,*
Wishful Thinking: A Seeker's ABC

CHAPTER 4

THE GIFT OF YOUR PASSIONS AND VALUES

Review and reflection

In a world suffering from a crisis of meaning, I am suggesting that a human person is incapable of sufficiently generating meaning in life. Whether it is meaning, purpose, love, hope, or salvation, these are realities that are both necessary for human existence and, at the same time, exceed our grasp. They can only be received as gifts from God. As God is moved to the periphery of our beliefs and imaginations in the postmodern world, we will find ourselves starving for what could be called "the bread of life" (John 6:35)—the Word God speaks that gives us life. And yet the bread of life is still given. God spoke and creation was called into existence, but not like a big clock meant to tick away for the rest of time while God stands idly by like an absentee landlord. Rather, creation is a dynamic tapestry of life and wonder, infused and filled with the presence of God. We, too, were called into being, called to join God in this world in a relationship of trust, called to till and keep the garden of creation. Made in the image of God, we were made to be curators of life and to do so in partnership with God who alone has the wisdom and goodness necessary for created life to be whole. The trajectory of creation and human existence lies in the loving hands of God, and their future will be the flourishing of life in its full amplitude. To be a part of this and to contribute toward this end is inherently meaningful.

But we need guidance on what it means to discern God's calling to me in my particularity and finitude. How and what does God want me to do? It starts with loving your neighbor in your daily vocational roles. It means paying attention to your story in a way that both reflects grace and bears it for others. Your own story can be a testimony to God's abiding presence and promise. And yet, the world is so full of possible directions, pursuits, and forks in the road. It's one thing to let our story unfold in the places we live our lives, but we are no passive passengers, for we have agency and decisions to make every day. What are the guardrails and boundaries that guide our daily lives? What are the realities and possibilities around us that stir within us like fuel that moves us into participation? That is what this chapter is about.

What is resonating from the previous chapter on your story?

_____

_____

_____

What loose ends or questions do you have?

_____

_____

_____

CHAPTER OVERVIEW

In this chapter, we will continue to explore the gifts from God that allow us to be both fully human and unique individuals. Specifically, you'll be asked to reflect on your core values and passions in the context of your relationship with God. The gift of values and passions is essential to helping us have meaning and purpose in life. As human beings, we are wired to accomplish those things we value and are passionate about. As we are discerning what God wants us to do in life, it will likely have a lot to do with these two factors. Passion means there is energy available for something to be done, while values will point us in a certain direction and within certain boundaries. These gifts—involving heart, mind, and will—assist greatly in helping us discern how God is calling us to partner with

God in the world. And the converse is true as well: our relationship with God and openness to God's movement in our lives will help us discern the values that really matter and the passions that nurture life. Indeed, it is the case that in this fallen world, our values and passions can be more a product of a life curved inward—incurvatus se—than a life extended outward for the sake of the neighbor.

In this chapter, we also continue our exploration of what it means to be a finite human being. In a world of infinite possibility, the gift of passions and values can both rouse and focus our energies for meaningful engagement. Discernment that our values and passions are in alignment with what God is up to in the world permits us to say yes to some things and no to others. The bottom line is that it matters which values and passions are being cultivated—namely, whether or not they're rooted in a theocentric (God-centered) perspective—but more on that later.

Introduction to the gift of values and passions

There are few gifts as powerful within human beings as the force of passion and conviction. Such motivational power as this usually comes out of our sense of values, of what's important in life. Few values arouse more passion than the pursuit of justice and fairness.

FILM CLIP

In the movie, *Spotlight*, we learn about the true story of a team of investigative journalists with The Boston Globe who investigate decades of clergy sexual abuse in the Catholic Church. The more they dig, the more they see a massive cover-up, which only feeds a growing sense that the problem at hand really, really matters. Their passion and unshakable sense of justice fuel their quest and guide their pursuit. In one key scene, as they uncover powerfully damning evidence about one priest, a member of the team passionately makes the case for going public. However, the leader of the investigative team is resolute about keeping a lid on it, taking aim instead at the much higher goal of dismantling the very system that engenders this kind of abuse. An intense argument ensues. Eventually, a small investigative team blew open an entire culture created to protect the guilty. Why? Because of passion and values.[1]

---

1 McCarthy, *Spotlight*, 1:35:02–1:38:07.

What motivates you and gets you out of bed in the morning? What stirs you to embrace a cause or pursuit, perhaps even risking life and limb to accomplish it?

LEARNING: PASSION AND VALUES ALIGNMENT

A DIVINE GIFT EASILY MISDIRECTED

The word *passion* has a long history from antiquity through the early Renaissance that rendered its meaning as something very broad, closer to the emotive aspect of being human.[2] And emotions and feelings have generally been seen to be in tension with matters of the spirit or reason, often as a lower expression of our humanity. Necessary and good, but lower. But there is another expression tied to the word passion that is not seen as lower, and it informs our contemporary understanding of passion. When we speak today of one's passions in life, we often mean those things or activities about which someone has "enthusiasm." Indeed, both words convey excitement and energy. Interestingly, the root word—or words— for enthusiasm are the Greek words, *en Theos*—which means "in God."[3] Another of its meanings in its Latin and Greek origins is "to be inspired or possessed by a god."[4] Such an understanding is also closely associated with the word ecstasy, a word often signifying a sensual experience, but originally—and most profoundly—was a word used to communicate a spiritual experience, even the direct experience of God.

Is it possible that enthusiasm in its purest form is the Spirit of God within us? I want to suggest that our passions are both signs of God's presence and gifts from God, so if we pay attention to our passions, we are also taking steps to discern how God might be calling us to partner with God. God knows that as human beings, we need to have purpose and meaning in our lives, which is virtually fuel to get out of bed and to engage life. This is the root of passion, that to which we are drawn because it gives us some measure of meaning. Passions, then, are signs of the Holy Spirit—the power of God at work in the world and in our hearts, stirring us to meaningful action.

---

2 For instance, Aristotle's understanding of human nature placed two kinds of "passions"—concupiscent and irascible—as being a lower nature than reason and will. St. Augustine connects disordered love with disordered passions.
3 Kise et. al, *Discover*, 30.
4 "Enthusiasm," lines 3-4.

However, passions that are cultivated from the wrong values or emotional needs do not result in meaningful action. For instance, any passion that leads one down a path of obsessive behavior or disregard for important callings and commitments may find themselves no longer in partnership with God but rather working at cross purposes with God. A person who is passionate about golf but fails to put boundaries on their time at the golf course may very well end up neglecting the most important relationships in their life. I recently watched the movie, *Nyad*,[5] about the famously driven marathon swimmer, Diana Nyad. There could be no better example of unbridled passion than Nyad's drive to swim from Cuba to Florida. It is at once remarkable, inspiring, and admirable—it would seem. Then again, *is it* admirable? At least in the film depiction, her passion for this accomplishment takes on a highly obsessive quality, causing her at times to disregard others' needs and collapse the entire meaning of her life to her success or failure at this superhuman feat. She believed there should be no limits placed on her from anyone, least of all herself. But is this a sustainable and healthy philosophy? If we truly think there are no limits to what we can do, perhaps our passion has deceived us into thinking we are no longer finite. And what purpose does it serve? I have no idea whether Nyad gives any credence to the idea of callings from God, but if that were the case, how would such a goal serve the common good—or at least the well-being of Nyad herself? I'm not suggesting that isn't possible, but the question needs to be raised.

The spark of energy that drives us to engage our mind, body, and soul with our neighbor and the world around us is good! And that most definitely includes athletic endeavors. But when our engagement lacks boundaries or thoughtful purpose, the gift of passion and the energy for life that God gives us is turned in on itself and fails to serve life. Passions can then be abused, distorted, and aligned with the wrong things. Passions or values cultivated to serve only the self or one's tribe while at the expense of others are not in alignment with God's vision for life. An obvious example would be a commonly held value to get what you can while you can. This value is entirely focused on the self and expresses the value of satiating one's appetite. If this is combined, for instance, with the passion of sexual drive or accumulating money or possessions, the results will likely disregard the needs of my neighbor in my headlong pursuit to consume—clear examples of incurvatus.

This is precisely why the raw energy of passion—for whatever pursuit—needs the guidance, guardrails, and telos (aim) of values—values rooted

---

5   Chin and Vasarhelyi, *Nyad*.

in convictions about what really matters, what is life-affirming, and what serves the common good. One may have a passion for leadership, but without the guiding values of servanthood and ethics, leadership can become a dangerous pursuit of sheer power. As such, values are commitments that shape our lives, guiding not only our passions but decisions of every kind. Values allow for the possibility of living a meaningful life because they point us in a direction that makes a difference, toward an end that matters. The value of honesty, for instance, matters because it insists that for life to flourish, we must be able to trust one another and the world we create together. And a trustworthy world cannot exist without honesty. Or, one might hitch their wagon to the value of equality. This matters because in a fallen world such as ours, we are prone to fashioning hierarchical social systems where the powerful take advantage of the weak. To fight for equality for everyone is a powerfully human act that honors the biblical witness that all human beings are made in the image of God!

Here we see the close affinity and symbiotic relationship between values and passions. Usually, what we're passionate about springs forth from what we value. We may become passionate about something because we've learned that it represents a valued principle to us. Then again, we may value something because we first felt passionate about it. Values and passions are powerful gifts that combine the energy and purpose to make a positive difference in the world.

SO MANY VALUES TO CHOOSE FROM

And yet even though many values are good, not all of them can be a priority for any given individual. There are simply far too many good and worthy values to choose from. For instance, consider the following list of values offered by one of many online values clarification tests:

Certainty, control, security, peace, health, discipline, job security, wealth, financial stability, pleasure, tradition, trust, privacy, accountability, challenge, adventure, variety, excitement, courage, curiosity, creativity, reputation, respect, authority, fame, authenticity, beauty, appreciation, acceptance, influence, popularity, uniqueness, love, family, honesty, loyalty, forgiveness, compassion, friendship, growth, passion, excellence, determination, success, independence, religion, wisdom, intelligence, competence, spirituality, inner harmony, ambition, contribution, equality, justice, meaningful work, teamwork, tolerance, commitment, ethics.[6]

When I look at this list, I'm overwhelmed, not only because there are so many, but because I agree that most of them are important. The trouble is, if you don't knock it down to a handful, but rather pretend to embrace them all, there's more than a good chance you'll end up only giving lip service to many of them. Here is where we are back to our finitude once again as creatures made by God. We must prioritize the most important values or fall victim to professing a multiplicity of values that we have little hope of fully embracing. Here's precisely where values become a vital resource and gift. Discerning with God what values in our lives are foundational gives our lives focus and definition. And once claimed, values give us the possibility for meaningful relationships with others who share our values.

There are two levels of value sorting to which one might attend. The first regards those values (and passions) that are a matter of taste and have a moral/ethical neutrality about them. In other words, they are values of preference, self-delineation, and self-care. These values are generated by the particularity of our unique story, personality, and those things that feed us, or that we simply like. While some might value being outside in the natural world whenever possible, others are drawn to urban life. While some value working in teams, others prefer to work individually. While some value spontaneity in their friends, others value predictability more. There are no right and wrong answers here, but part of knowing yourself is knowing what you value and what's important to you. These values that are more personal are so critical to discerning our callings from God. Remember, God seeks to put your particular person and what you value in alignment with God's leading.

The second tier of values is more ethically and morally weighted—and more universal. Values like justice, ethics, honesty, trust, and equality all presuppose a broader community of people and compel us to act in such a way that you actively seek their interests. These values are in a natural tension with values such as fame, popularity, wealth, and pleasure—values that are not inherently wrong at all, but generally pursued for the sake one's of own interests or self-advancement.

However, this leads us to a big fork in the road when it comes to values: What are your meta-values—the values that guide all others? Western

---

6   "Personal Values Free Online Test."

culture is deeply individualistic and consumer-driven, and hence, heavily predisposes its citizens to cultivate values that lead toward the satisfaction and development of the self. Not self as a means to a broader purpose—like serving humanity or taking care of the planet—but self as a proper end. Self-interest can indeed become a meta-value that frames and guides all other values. Specifically, when the value of self-advancement or self-interest has ultimate value, we are squarely back to incurvatus se, the glorification of the self or its social corollary, the tribe. When this happens, people—and their tribes—turn against one another in a sociology of conflict and division.

It must be said with no ambivalence that values framed by the meta-value of self-interest fail to create a sustaining meaning or purpose. Here, values only drive one deeper into emptiness.

But the other meta-value is love. While love doesn't exclude self-interest—and certainly not self-care—it is firmly established according to a different gravitational pole: the needs of my neighbor, and the common good. The meta-narrative of love asks not: How can I advance myself? but rather, What is God seeking to do in our world? This value orientation leads to life that is whole and flourishing not only for self but for others. Considerable anthropological research shows us that as an evolved species, human beings don't easily think—and especially act—this way, however.[7] We have a hard time not placing self or group interest at the forefront, often at the expense of the other. Conversely, to show love for or solidarity with the other is often to incur the wrath of one's own group that seems predisposed to devalue the other. Fortunately, Christians have a North Star: the limitless love of God in Jesus Christ, the antecedents of which are expressed in the Ten Commandments and the witness of the Old Testament prophets. The echoes of this kind of love can be hugely inspirational, in history or fiction.

The pivot to values rooted in love

FILM CLIP

In the movie, *on the Waterfront*, the mob runs the longshoreman union in a 1950s New York harbor and is guilty of extortion and racketeering. The result is the fleecing of the workers while the bosses live in luxury. Those who speak up or are willing to testify are quickly—and permanently—silenced. The story is

7 For instance, in Jonathan Haidt's The Righteous Mind, he explores the hard-wired tribal and self-interested nature of human beings

60

about two individuals in particular who respond to a higher calling: to put their lives on the line by letting their growing passion
and clarifying values speak loudly and clearly. In one scene, an
"accident" at the docks takes the life of a longshoreman who had
shown a willingness to testify against the mob. The local priest
(played by Karl Malden) steps in with a fierce passion calling
out the corrupt dehumanizing values of organized crime while
at the same time reminding everyone that what they witnessed
wasn't an accident but an execution. The priest spellbindingly
proclaims that such a death as this is a sign that Christ is there
with everyone gathered, sharing in that execution, and testifying
to a kingdom where its constitutive values foster life, not death.[8]

THE TEN COMMANDMENTS ARE ALL ABOUT LOVE

Often in values inventories, the word love is listed as one among many.
If we are to understand the Ten Commandments correctly, however—as
I noted in Chapter 2—they are all about one thing: love. In other words,
to love our neighbor and love God means precisely what the commandments describe. For the Christian, the mother ship to which all other
values come and go is love. As a reminder, it must be clarified again that
love as a governing value is not a feeling—as our culture would define it—
but rather a commitment. Love in its purest form is *agape*, quite simply
the commitment to speak and act in such a way that the best interests of
my neighbor are served so that my neighbor's life might thrive. There is
nothing wrong with values that are aimed at self-fulfillment and pleasure,
and yet these values must align with—and never supersede—the values
that exhort us to seek the common good of our neighbors.

And I would be remiss to not point out that the first three Commandments are about loving God. These Commandments are so important
because they provide the anchor for loving one's neighbor. If we worship
and love God, then we adopt God's vision and values, which are about
the human community, not merely myself. As people of faith, how do we
honor and live out the value of loving God above all else and committing
to what God stands for? When we do love God, we love who God loves!
The Ten Commandments make clear that our chief concerns in life are
located *outside* of ourselves, in God and neighbor. The values of love
of God and love of neighbor are the meta-values that guide our daily
existence.

---

8 Kazan, *Waterfront*, 50:30—58:55.

But again, the implicit values that issue from the meta-value of love are then in serious tension with the culture around us; a culture that urges us to glorify the self with expressions like "You gotta do what's best for you." One can easily live this way and then tack on charity and religion to demonstrate their well-roundedness. It's the difference between *my* goals and *God's* goals for God's creation. The question then, as we are discerning our values, is what values are consistent with love—not love as a feeling but a commitment and worldview?

The Ten Commandments are one way to look at all this. And then there is God's promise of the kingdom that is to come, vividly described by the prophets and embodied in Jesus of Nazareth. We will discuss the kingdom of God in more detail in a later chapter, but it is highly pertinent to this discussion as well. There are essential values that emerge when we consider the kingdom of God.

VALUES OF GOD'S KINGDOM COME

The kingdom of God is God's promised future and vision of abundant life for all. It is distinguished by its universal perspective that transcends boundaries of self-interest and tribalism. This is a vision and set of values that is impossible for humans to pursue on their own as they (we) are irredeemably curved in on self and tribal interests. Only the presence and agency of our redeeming God in Jesus of Nazareth has shown us what the kingdom looks like; only Jesus can free us to embrace such values seriously.

What core values do we find in Jesus and the prophets? Kingdom values are exemplified in Jesus's famous quoting of Isaiah:

> The Spirit of the Lord is upon me
> because he has anointed me to bring good news to the poor.
>   He has sent me to proclaim release to the captives
>   and recovery of sight to the blind
> to let the oppressed go free,
> to proclaim the year of the Lord's favor.
>   (Luke 4:17–21)

This prophecy is based on the Year of the Lord's Favor—the year of Jubilee—a proclamation of liberation for those whose lives have been bound and diminished by a cruel world of hierarchy and greed. Its under-girding values are social and economic justice for those on the margins, forgiveness of debts, inclusion for the disenfranchised, healing for the broken, and abundance for everyone. Additionally in the prophetic writings about the kingdom of God, we find the value of hospitality to the stranger rather than rejection (Heb 13:1-12); peacemaking replacing conflict (Mic 4:3); reconciliation whereby all peoples come together in unity (Isa 43:9). All these values are summarized by loving one's neighbor. God calls us to align our lives and our passions with these kingdom values.

As Frederick Buechner reminds us, God calls us to a place where our deep gladness (passion) is aligned (values) with the world's needs. And that amounts to a prayer: that what is stirring in our hearts and moves us to act is aligned in such a way as to speak to a world in need.

ASSESSMENT TOOLS

There are many easy-to-use assessment tools available online to help you sort out your core values. The values inventory I listed earlier can be found on the website Personalvalu.es and has a free online test.[9] This inventory has generated a long list of values to choose from, which forces one to choose and discern. Also, a highly respected online assessment (not free, though) is offered by the Barrett Values Centre.[10] They provide a detailed report on your assessment with suggestions for your personal development.

SUMMARY

For finite human beings who need purpose and direction in life, the gift of values and passions is vital. They are discovered and discerned as we journey through life and our unique story and personality emerge. Given the countless options each person has for direction in life, passions provide the energy to act forcefully, while values provide the necessary boundaries and guardrails for our passions and all our actions. Etymologically, passion and its close cousin, enthusiasm, suggest an energy that is akin to a divine spark. When aligned with the right values, our passions are indeed gifts from God that invite us to work alongside God toward a more trustworthy world. Meanwhile, values can be both matters of personal preference and interest or have much more ethical and universal implications. Here is where a critical fork in the road emerges, where we must choose our culture or God's vision and calling for us. Whereas our

9   "Personal Values Free Online Test."
10 "Personal Values Assessment."

culture usually fosters values that seek the glorification of the self, God calls us to embrace and live out values that are based on the meta-value of love. The Ten Commandments are all about it, the prophets described it, and Jesus embodied it: a world based on the love of God and neighbor. This is the only way human existence can finally work! Values that primarily serve self or clan do not create sustaining meaning or a better world.

In Chapter 5, we turn to another gift with great potential to clarify our callings in the world: our unique personality.

Reflection and conversation: processing what you've learned

REFLECTION ON MY VALUES

1. As you've reflected on your most important values—whether by taking an online inventory or just making a list—what emerges as your top eight to ten values?

_____

_____

_____

_____

_____

_____

_____

_____

_____

2. Is there a theme or pattern in the values that you chose? What can you learn about yourself from this list?

_____

_____

_____

3. If the people who know you best listed what they thought your top eight values were, do you think they would come up with the same list? Why or why not?

_____

_____

_____

4. Is there a good alignment between your top eight values and your life (work, volunteering, family, leisure, etc.)? Or not?

_____

_____

_____

5. Which of your values align well with your understanding of the kingdom of God?

_____

_____

_____

REFLECTING ON MY PASSIONS

1. Name three to five passions you have.

_____

_____

_____

_____

_____

2. Which passions get the most time for expression and development? Do you have a passion or two that is underdeveloped?

_____

_____

_____

3. Which of your passions feels like it might be en Theos—namely, that God is (or could be) involved? Why do you feel that way?

_____

_____

_____

4. Which passion is best aligned with kingdom values or the Ten Commandments?

_____

_____

_____

5. Do you see any potential new alignments between your values and passions that have not been previously paired?

_____

_____

_____

6. If we don't value something or feel passionate about it, it may well be the case that we need to say *no*. What is something you need to say no to?

_____

_____

_____

Wrap-up

What questions do you have from Chapter 4?

_____

_____

_____

What takeaways do you have?

_____

_____

_____

The meeting of two personalities is like the contact of two chemical substances; if there is any reaction, both are transformed.

—*Carl Jung, Modern Man in Search of a Soul*

CHAPTER 5

THE GIFT OF YOUR PERSONALITY

Review and reflection

We've been unpacking elements of a meaningful life. Building on the foundational bedrock of trust in the God who made us and loves us, we are called into a partnership with the triune God in the *missio Dei*. This mission entails many callings, all of them calibrated according to the uniqueness of each person's particularity—the places we live, our story, the values and passions that guide and propel us. And all of our callings are for two purposes: love of God and love of neighbor. As reverberations of God's love for us, these two loves round out the fullness of human life. This is how we become fully human. For all the striving and reaching of the modern, "liberated," human being, fancying ourselves self-sufficient and independent from God turns us into the proverbial Icarus,[1] and our true potential crashes and burns.

In the current chapter, we continue our journey through the many gifts God has given us. Few are more potent than the distinct presence,

---

1 A Greek mythological figure, the son of Daedalus who to escape imprisonment flies using artificial wings but falls into the sea and drowns when the wax of his wings melts as he flies too near the sun. This allusion refers to someone or a people who are over-ambitious in their aspirations and pay for it with their demise.

potential, and impact of your personality. But first, let's check in with what's resonating.

What is resonating with you from Chapter 4, where we examined the guiding light of your values and passions?

_____

_____

_____

What questions do you have about Chapter 4?

_____

_____

_____

CHAPTER OVERVIEW

"Well, it takes all kinds!" This expression is usually an editorial comment about someone (or more than one) who has shown themselves to be somewhat eccentric or at least different. The implication is that it takes all kinds of people to make a community of people work. And indeed, that is true!

This chapter is all about identifying and celebrating your unique personality as an essential part of the diverse social economy of God. Despite the relative values we place on some personalities over others, all personalities bear our creator's purposeful touch (but indeed suffer distortion in a broken world). That means each of us processes and interacts with the world a little differently, and that's a good thing! Diversity in personalities can make any community not only more interesting but also healthier and more productive. But in this world, where we rank personalities according to popularity or magnetism, we easily lose sight of the importance of the whole range of personalities necessary to strengthen families, teams, and communities. As a result, we often adopt a certain _persona_ in certain social situations because we believe that persona will be advantageous to us, even though it may not be who we really are. We need to be reminded, though, that it's not only the star personalities—the extroverts, entertainers, and natural-born leaders—who have an important place in the public and private dimensions of human community. It's also the introverts, salt-of-the-earth types of people, and those who are more likely to follow than lead, or to lead quietly.

Indeed, Jung was correct that the meeting of two personalities (regardless of their nature) always carries the potential for transformation for either party. This is because human beings are essentially social beings who need and are changed by each other. Instead of being isolated individual units, we are indelibly shaped and changed by the presence of others, and they are by the presence of us. In fact, theologian Jürgen Moltmann has famously said that an individual is not a person. A person is defined by relationship, while an individual is not. "Seeing ourselves as individuals creates the illusion our lives are not connected to others and implies, we are not dependent on others."[2] It is our calling from God to let our personality be a life-enhancing asset in our relationships with others.

Introduction to the gift of your personality

When my wife and I started dating, it was fun and sometimes challenging to discover our differences and commonalities. Our common ground included our values and our faith. But our personalities are fairly different. Depending on the situation, this difference can be delightful, amusing, or occasionally, irritating. For instance, we both enjoyed dates when we went to a movie. Often, our taste in movies even matched! But the big difference was après cinema (after the movie). Being a reflective sort of person, I was used to discussing a movie after I saw it, analyzing it for its thesis, its subtle meanings, and its symbolism. Heidi, on the other hand, thought I was analyzing it to death. "The movie was great," she would say. "Now, how about we move on to the next thing!"

Two different personalities. I linger and dwell. She moves on. Thankfully, we've made it work for us. Sometimes opposite personalities can work in a very complementary way.

If you're a *Star Trek* fan, it's fun to compare the colorful tapestry of different personalities from the show. On the one hand, you have Captain Kirk, the emotional, instinctive risk taker, and on the other hand, his ultimate counterbalance: Admiral Spock. Unemotional, analytical, logical, and cautious. Together they made quite a team because they respected each other and understood that each other's contributions were important and

---

2 Moltmann quoted by Elton, *Journeying*, 133.

necessary for the team. On a much larger scale, this is how an authentic, God-centered community works as well. It recognizes the gift of diversity within a community, and one of the ways diversity is manifest is through personality—whether one is an optimist or a pessimist, sunny or stormy, loud or quiet, cautious or impulsive. The world needs a rich palette of personalities. For instance, sometimes the world even needs a Debbie Downer when darkness and negation must be tended to. One particular film captured this brilliantly.

FILM CLIP

In the animated movie, *Inside Out*, we explore the inner world of an adolescent girl named Riley who is in the midst of the very difficult transition of her family moving. The premise of the movie is to show the interplay of the five core emotions experienced by Riley. The five emotions—joy, sadness, disgust, fear, and anger—are portrayed as characters in themselves within Riley's psyche. The message of the movie is how essential each emotion is in a well-rounded and healthy personality—even sadness. As scenes unfold with each emotion, we realize that we are not only witnessing isolated emotions at play but also personality types.

The scene I'd like to highlight takes place within Riley's inner world as she is growing up, a landscape rich with the very detail one would expect from the inner life of a growing, changing adolescent. As she grows, Riley leaves behind some of her childhood memories and imaginary characters—characters who are nonetheless very real in Riley's world. One of those characters, Bing Bong, is grieving because he knows that his place in Riley's psyche is fading. In one very poignant scene, Bing Bong is distraught. It is then that joy and sadness—each represented as a character—attempt to console him. One fails and one succeeds. You would think that it was Joy who would be just what Bing Bong needed but you would be wrong. Sadness is the character who provides the empathy needed to cheer up Bing Bong. Sadness, you see, is not afraid to let Bing Bong simply be sad and join him in that space with her own sadness.[3]

Again, in the movie, these characters represent emotions in a girl's psyche, but they also are personalities who each have moments when they are meant to shine. Just like us! Obviously, there are times when a

---

3 Doctor, *Inside Out*, 47:04–49:39.

half-glass-full type of personality is much needed to encourage others. And there is also a time when the glass that is only half full (or less!) must be acknowledged and honored. It is a bit like the rhythms of life expressed in the iconic passage from Ecclesiastes:

> ... a time to weep,
>   and a time to laugh;
>   a time to mourn,
>   and a time to dance.
>   (Eccl 3:4)

Certain personalities help us weep and mourn while others help us laugh and dance! And so, it is with all of the personalities that God has given to each of us. They are all given for a purpose—the purpose of building up human spirits and communities.

LEARNING: LOADS OF PERSONALITY

It is surely the case that any community, team, or household needs to have sufficient gifts, resources, aptitudes (and emotions!) present for that community to work. We will later examine how important each person's natural gifts and abilities are for the common good. But arguably nothing is more important than the gift of one's personality. What's being explored now is not simply a skill one brings to the table for the betterment of the community. This is the sum of the parts, the totality of *who someone is*, the way they're wired, and the subtle qualities that make someone who they are in real time. Our true personality is to be contrasted with the various *personas*—masks—we may put on or be tempted to wear to project a certain personality that we think will be advantageous to us for some reason.

Because God has created me, including my unique personality, we can be confident about *who we are*. And because God has justified us, we have been freed to unapologetically be ourselves. Our guilt has been washed away by forgiveness. Our shame and inadequacy have been vanquished by God's declaration that each of us has inestimable value to God. Indeed, Luke writes eloquently about the value each of us has to God, reminding us that "... even the hairs on your head are all counted" (Luke 12:7). Our oft-repeated struggle with meaninglessness has been replaced by the presence of a God who is at work in the forgotten corners of our lives and world, who even invites us to join God there as a partner. Our loneliness has been transformed by the promise of a community to which we belong—a community that will last forever. We have freedom and we have a place, and need not ever question the intrinsic value of our particular, God-given persona. Our personality, with all its quirks, capacities, and shortcomings, is a gift to the world. As the famous uncredited ghetto poet once wrote: "God made me and God don't make no junk!"

THE INFLATED VALUE OF A WINNING PERSONALITY

And yet we do question the value of our own person in this world because certain personalities are praised while other personalities are underappreciated or even considered a liability. But the truth is, every personality is praiseworthy for what it can bring to relationships and communities. And on the flip side, the very thing that makes a personality praiseworthy (or, at least helpful) can also be a liability if self-awareness is lacking. Ancient Chinese philosopher Lao Tzu insightfully wrote:

> He who knows does not speak.
>
> He who speaks does not know.[4]

We all recognize this! Often, those who have important insight or wisdom are not inclined to speak because they might be introverts. If only they would speak up more! Meanwhile, for those who are strongly inclined to speak, their many words sometimes outstrip their content. In other words, some folks seem to have a need to speak even if they have nothing to say. And so, it is important that the probing reflections that introverts may have on account of their naturally rich inner life do not go to waste by always remaining unexpressed. Likewise, the capacity that extroverts and Type A individuals typically have to effortlessly engage in conversation, discussion, and persuasion must be tempered sometimes by choosing to listen and reflect rather than generating more words.

That said, it is hard to maintain a balanced view of personality types in modern American culture. In modern American culture, personality has become less about substance and more about self-promotion. In her book, *Quiet*, author Susan Cain describes how American culture in the twentieth century took an interesting turn. While nineteenth century American culture praised, above all else, character and integrity in individuals, the twentieth century would see the rise of *personality*—but in a way that has slowly downgraded the importance of character and integrity. Andrew Carnegie's book, *How to Win Friends and Influence*

---

4 "Lao Tzu Quotes."

People became a huge bestseller. In a burgeoning capitalist nation, the importance of the sale and the deal maker grew rapidly. The rise of movie stars, rock stars, and celebrities emphasized star power and attractive personas. Compared with earlier times, more emphasis was now placed on one's ability to sell oneself than on grounding oneself.[5]

Along with the rise of the importance of personality came the rise of certain coveted traits: winsomeness, wit, extroversion, and charisma. We all know that our culture defines "charisma" as the quality of being charmingly persuasive, yet the word charisma is derived from the Greek word *charism*, a gift given by the Holy Spirit to Christians. This gift is roughly synonymous with a spiritual gift, and we will explore this much more in Part II. However, it's worth pointing out that the original meaning and use of the word charism embraced a broad spectrum of gifts, not just those associated with charm. This is just an example of how words evolve in cultures that reflect the values of that culture. In the case of American culture, what is valued is too narrow, while what is devalued is too broad.

Cain goes on to describe the thesis of her book: that extroverts are valued more than introverts in a world such as ours. It is quickly assumed by many that extroverts make the world go round, that they are the ones who lead us, take charge, get things done, make deals when needed, and so forth. And so—according to conventional wisdom and more than a few workshop retreats—introverts are well served to become more like extroverts if they want success. Yet Cain reminds us that this is clearly not the case. Introverts are just as likely to be leaders in all sectors—and just as effective—as extroverts. In fact, introverts succeed in many fields and endeavors precisely *because* they are introverts. The space and privacy that introverts seek, the openness to let others talk, the patience to reflect and analyze—these are often difficult for extroverts. And it is these qualities that can facilitate great success. The point Cain makes is not that introverts are better than extroverts, but that they are equally valuable for human community. The world needs both extroverts and introverts, and each personality type brings gifts to the communities of which they are a part.[6]

As is the case with introverts, so it is with personality traits of all kinds. While some personalities are undoubtedly more magnetic and attention-grabbing, it is a complete mistake to attach more value to that kind of person for that reason. It is often the unsung heroes, the salt-of-the-earth, steady and thoughtful people who hold things together in families,

---

5 Cain, *Quiet*, 19-31
6 Cain, *Quiet*.

teams, and communities. Sometimes the person who doesn't draw a lot of attention also creates space for mutual support, teamwork, and a spirit of interdependence. And perhaps empathy where empathy is desperately needed.

If it sounds like I'm being too hard on the charismatic extroverts of the world, I don't mean to be! But the truth is, their personas are rarely questioned in our world and perhaps they are less likely to feel undervalued. Yet for the many individuals out there who do not fit this description, inferiority complexes abound. In the fullness of God's creation, this need not be the case.

PERSONALITY IN THE BIBLE

The Bible gives us a colorful palette of characters with quite diverse personalities. And to the credit of the biblical writers, they do not whitewash the liabilities of key characters, just as they appropriately celebrate their contributions to human history. For instance, the most famous disciple of Jesus is Peter, and for good reason. He is a natural leader, boldly speaking up where others sit back in deference. Indeed, in Matt 16:18 Jesus, declares that Peter is the *petros* (which means "rock") upon which Jesus will build the church—an allusion in part to the character and passion that Peter possesses. And yet his boldness is also a liability, or can be, for we also know that Peter is impetuous and prone to going out too far on a limb that exceeds his understanding or what his own will is capable of. It is a profound word of grace that just as Jesus recognizes the pitfalls Peter's personality will create, he also recognizes its value for this nascent movement called Christianity. With the gift of forgiveness, all of us can take heart in the fact that whatever blindsides there may be in my personality are outweighed by the goodness and value that God invested in who I am.

There is another critical aspect here, and it reflects a Protestant perspective. Since Christ's Church consists of countless human lives—present and past—the metaphor of a rock that Jesus used also represents the everyman and woman upon whose faith the church is built. And this means that the *rock* is actually about a multitude of personalities—necessary personalities to make up something as solid as a rock. So, what if you're not like the rest? That's a good thing because your perspective makes the body of Christ that much more expansive, rich, and capable. This discussion, of course, anticipates the major New Testament theme of the complementary parts of the body of Christ (I Cor 12:14-27).

Or consider the example of another disciple: doubting Thomas. He, of course, became famous for his doubts about the reports of Jesus's resurrection. "Unless I see the mark of the nails in his hands, and put my finger in the mark of the nails and my hand in his side, I will not believe," declared Thomas to his fellow disciples (John 20:25). Now, a doubting predisposition like this can be a hindrance to having faith. It can characterize individuals who are reluctant to step up when necessary. And yet a person who is cautious like Thomas—measuring twice before cutting once (as the saying goes)—can become a forceful advocate upon conversion. Having navigated doubts and an extensive vetting process, the doubting Thomases among us are capable of courageous, unwavering conviction. Such was the case with Thomas, who took the good news of Jesus far beyond the boundaries of the other disciples. In fact, Thomas founded the Christian Church in India and was martyred there. Yes, if a naturally skeptical person allows doubt to color everything in their life, this kind of personality can be an albatross. But suppose someone uses their skepticism and inclination to doubt as an asset—asking questions, considering all options carefully, and deliberately entertaining possibilities. In that case, there is always a place for this kind of personality.

To introduce my next biblical character, I give you the fictional TV character, James McGill, a.k.a., Saul Goodman, from *Better Call Saul*.[7] The portrayal of this character is given rich and wonderful nuance. He is charming and witty, with a good heart and intrinsic sense of justice—particularly for the underdogs and marginalized of this world. And yet, he also has a slippery quality, a predisposition to bend the rules and con others. In short, he is a delightfully complex character who is very human. One finds oneself cheering him on one minute and groaning in disapproval the next!

We see this same kind of nuance in Jacob. Like McGill, Jacob was a wheeler/dealer, a schemer and deceiver, who also proves to have big dreams, a big imagination, and a big heart. Most famous for stealing the firstborn's birthright from his twin brother Esau (Gen 27), Jacob was downright unethical. And yet after stealing the birthright that belonged to his brother and fleeing for his life in the desert, Jacob experienced a grace-filled visitation from God—for which he knew he was not worthy—and allowed it to shape his life henceforth. It turned out that Jacob's wily ways and rich imagination could be readily subjected to more life-giving purposes, like, for instance, being blessed to become a blessing to all the families in the world; and being renamed *Israel* by God on the banks

---

7 Gilligan, *Better Call Saul.*

of the river Jabbok, a name that would also become the name of all the descendants of Jacob/Israel.

Israel means *one who struggles with God,* and that is precisely Jacob's personality in a nutshell. Jacob had just finished a mystical wrestling match with God and this encounter epitomized Jacob's contrarian, rogue nature. It also came to symbolize the very nature and personality, if you will, of the Hebrew people, a contrarian, stiff-necked people who were difficult for God to shepherd and lead. Why would God ever work with someone like Jacob, who wanted to wrestle with God? Or why choose a stiff-necked people like the Hebrews? Indeed, both of these characterizations can mean *resistant* to God's leading and that is not a good thing. However, they can also mean a combination of skeptical, questioning, stubborn, and independent, all of which can be very helpful qualities. Like Thomas, these qualities can signal both a certain level of difficulty along with the need to process and work through things. When that happens, one has the possibility of being stubborn about the right things and having the capacity for conviction, as opposed to being wishy-washy.

Or perhaps a further clue to God's choosing a stiff-necked people who struggle with God lies in Matthew 10:16. When Jesus sends his followers into the world to carry on his mission, he memorably tells them to be "wise as serpents and innocent as doves." Interesting advice, obviously reflecting the need to be sufficiently wily in a dog-eat-dog world while also bearing witness to a message of faith, hope, and love. We could say that Jacob had the wise-as-serpents part covered! Someone like Jacob could get things done in this world by negotiating, cutting deals, and perhaps even playing hardball when necessary. As necessary as someone like this is, they also need other voices to inform and guide them: voices of conscience and compassion. It would be up to others who were gentler and more innocent to round out the team.

Finally, we consider the personality of the most famous woman in the Bible: Mary, the mother of Jesus. Dominick Albano, who writes for The Catholic Telegraph, has written about the personality of Mary using the Myers-Briggs personality assessment tool.[8] First of all, Mary appears to be an introvert. Albano reasons that while an extrovert processes thoughts and feelings externally, an introvert usually doesn't want attention and keeps things inside. Twice in Luke's Gospel there are references to Mary's decidedly internal processing (verses 19 and 51) as she ponders the lofty and mysterious nature of her son, Jesus. Albano continues, observing that

---

8 Albano, "Mary's Myers-Briggs."

Mary seems to interact with the world around her intuitively, through her heart and feelings. This is in contrast to someone who is more logically based, taking in objective data points from their world and working it through from a logical point of view. Finally, rather than being the kind of person who needs to be in control and know the whole plan ahead of time, Mary lives in faith, not knowing, but trusting nonetheless. The result, if one uses a Myers-Briggs analysis, is an Introvert (I), an Intuitive (N), a Feelings (F), and Perceiving (P) based person. Mary is an INFP. Albano concludes, "Those who are INFP tend to be quiet, introspective, and extremely caring and creative. Empathy is usually among their greatest characteristics, and others describe INFPs as contemplative and kind. Does this sound like the Mary you know?"[9] Does this sound like the kind of person God would choose to bear the Son of God to the world?

When God made the astounding move to weave human stories with God's story, human personalities suddenly took on more significance than ever. God engages human agency in carrying out God's purposes, and that means our personalities (and all our gifts) are brought to the fore in creating a more trustworthy, faith-filled, and loving world.

WHAT IS YOUR PERSONALITY?

All personalities given by God in creation are unique and have something valuable to offer to human community. It must be pointed out, however, that all of our personalities have been compromised and distorted by the broken context in which we live in this world. This means that sometimes our personality—in this world's version—may hinder what love requires in a given situation. Discernment is needed to allow God to use our personality as a vehicle for love. But in some cases, a God-given personality may have become so seriously distorted by a broken social situation or mental illness that the personality itself is rendered harmful and an instrument of evil. The sociopath or malignant narcissist is an example of a personality damaged almost beyond repair (at least by human methods) with little—if any—redeeming value. But such are the inevitabilities of the fallen world in which we live. Thankfully, this is not the case for most people!

So, what's your personality? As you perhaps know already, there are many useful personality inventories out there—many of them available online free of charge. I would recommend two of them. The first is the very well-known MBTI (Myers-Briggs Type Inventory, sometimes referred to as the

---

9 Albano, "Mary's Myers-Briggs," lines 63-65.

"Jung personality test"). The inventory identifies sixteen basic personality types using four sets of polarities around key personality aspects, such as introvert/extrovert, for instance.[10] There are many options for taking this inventory online, but at least one is free and available at 16personalities. com.[11] Second, Enneagram is a very well-respected tool for personality assessments. Again, many online options are available, including a free test at EnneagramTest.com.[12] An introduction to both of these assessments and others is available at personality.com. Hopefully, as you reflect on your unique personality, you will see it as a gift from God be celebrated, not lamented. For while your personality will not be all things to all people, it can indeed be a means through which God is at work touching the lives around you in life-affirming ways. Part of recognizing the gift of personality is learning to be humble enough to accept the limits of your personality. That said, your personality, whatever it may be, is a gift to you and your neighbor. It is up to each of us to explore what that looks like and how it is lived out!

In the next chapter, we will turn to explore something that is closely related to personality and often emerges from it: your God-given natural abilities. These abilities are closely related to personality precisely because our personality is fertile soil for certain kinds of abilities that we might bring to the table. For instance, an INFP (like Mary) is already on a path that is conducive to being an artist or musician, simply because that person is wired a certain way. As we shall see, it is critically important that people learn how to build on their strengths, and predispositions (and yes, personality!) to maximize their giftedness. The other option, of course, is something many will quickly recognize: focus on your weaknesses—whatever you may lack—rather than what you already do well. While there is some merit to this, it can also quickly become a harmful detour.

---

10 "Myers-Briggs Type Indicators."
11 "Free Personality Test."
12 "Enneagram Personality Test."

SUMMARY

We've reviewed the giftedness and diversity of our personalities as reflections of the unique creations we all are. Whereas many labor under the notion that their personality is deficient or less valuable than that of others, vocational theology asserts the equal value of all personality types as important elements of a healthy human community. The qualifier here is what a fallen world can do to distort our God-given personalities, co-opting them for the detriment of life, rather than its upbuilding. And yet scripture and history have taught us that God works through the broken and flawed persons that we all are, personalities included! From within God's blessed order of creation and power of redemption, God is calling each of us to discern how it is that our unique personality can be utilized to not only affirm the goodness of our own life but to enrich the life of our neighbor and community. The truth is, whether one is more analytical or social by nature, introverted or extroverted, head or heart-driven, in-the-moment or a careful planner, all of these different orientations can be pathways to creating a more trustworthy, loving, and hopeful world. The fact that these orientations are always in complex combinations within each person's personality only enhances the power and potential of any given personality to enter a situation and give life. This makes our capacity to experience meaning deeply personal.

Reflection and conversation: processing what you've learned

1. Which of the four biblical characters discussed above (Peter, Thomas, Jacob, Mary) are you most like? How so?

_____

_____

_____

2. What sort of relationship have you had historically with your *personality*? Has it been a rocky relationship or harmonious one, one of acceptance and embrace or striving to be someone else you would rather be or think you should be?

_____

_____

_____

3. What do you like about your personality?

_____

_____

_____

4. Are there parts of your personality that you may have underestimated or underappreciated?

_____

_____

_____

5. Which parts of your personality are being honored right now in your life and given time and space to flourish?

_____

_____

_____

6. Are there parts of your personality that you might be uncomfortable with? Why is that, do you think? How can you learn to celebrate that part of you?

_____

_____

_____

7. Which parts of your personality are *not* being honored adequately in your life now—at work, at play, or in social relationships? How might you change that?

_____

_____

_____

8. How does your unique personality fit best into a community— like your faith community? How about your friendship circle? Your family?

_____

_____

_____

Take a moment to give thanks for exactly who you are. Ask God to help you embrace all of yourself, to embody that self with no regrets, but rather seek to fully be who God made you to be.

Wrap up

What questions do you have about Chapter 5?

_____

_____

_____

What is one takeaway from this chapter?

_____

_____

_____

God has already revealed His will to us
concerning our vocation and Mission,
by causing it to be 'written in our members.'
We are to begin deciphering our unique
Mission by studying our talents and skills
and more importantly which ones (or one)
we most rejoice to use.

—*Richard Bolles, What Color is your Parachute?*

You cannot be anything you want to be—
but you can be a lot more of who you
already are.

—*Tom Rath, StrengthsFinder 2.0*

CHAPTER 6

THE GIFT OF YOUR NATURAL ABILITIES

Review and reflection

We are exploring what a meaningful existence looks like in the world envisioned by God. Increasingly, this is no longer the starting point for how meaning and purpose are defined by our postmodern culture. In the current and unfortunate evolution of the human conception of itself, we each create (or attempt to) our own brand, meaning, and relevance in life. So, we begin with our particularity as the center and starting point of our world, perhaps alter it with a chosen persona, and then expand and project this version of ourselves out into the world. This quest for meaning is an echo chamber and leaves us wearily trudging through our days.

In stark contrast, vocational theology starts broadly with the presupposition that, as the creator of our world, God is at the center, God is the starting point, and we are members of a vast community of created life. Our creator, out of love, has established a relationship with this world—and with each of us—to nourish life so that life in its many forms may thrive. This is where meaning, purpose, and relevance come from—from outside ourselves through a relationship with God! Trusting in the benevolence of God, we are called to till and keep the garden of creation in a partnership with the God who creates anew continually. This constitutes a major part of God's missio Dei: joining with the very creatures created in the image of God to keep and co-create a more trustworthy, loving, life-filled and God-aware world. As such, in our very particularity and individuality we are gifted for this life-affirming task. God indeed works through our unfolding story and relationships, through our personality and what we've learned to value. Which brings us to our God-given abilities that distinguish us.

What is resonating with you from Chapter 5, where we examined personality?

_____

_____

_____

What questions do you have?

_____

_____

_____

Do you feel nudged in any particular direction as a result of your reflections thus far?

_____

_____

_____

CHAPTER OVERVIEW

In the previous chapter, we examined the gift of personality, how God created you *as a person* to interact with the world (and people) around you. In this chapter, we will consider the natural abilities God has given you. Such capacities are both clues to identifying some of our callings and tools that help us carry them out. And in light of the ever-expanding possibilities for how we spend our time in the current society of self-made men and women, discernment is all the more crucial. To better understand what God might be calling you to do, it's important to understand not only what kind of personality you have, but what specific gifts you *have* and do *not* have. This is especially true when the current cultural zeitgeist misleads us into thinking we can be anything we choose to be, i.e., that we are practically gods! Well, the real God has not equipped us to be anything we want to be. But God does equip us for certain callings that align with our personality and natural abilities. And rather than focusing on the misguided strategy of trying to become someone you are not, I believe God calls us to lean into who we are—to celebrate our personality and strengths and develop them, for it is precisely our natural strengths that reveal a pathway forward.

On this pathway, we are invited to consider how our giftedness might be utilized for the sake of our neighbor. How might my natural abilities be utilized not merely for my own pleasure (certainly a worthy pursuit in itself), but also to benefit those around me? This is the major point of this book: *we are blessed to be a blessing!* These were the two movements of God's love that animated and led the leaders of the Israelites and the early Christian Church. A man named Luther picked them up, made them the twin pillars of his theology, but enriched and deepened these pillars as justification and vocation—God's unconditional love *for* me and *through* me to others.

Introduction to the gift of your natural abilities

We begin by examining a historical figure who struggled to synchronize his world-class ability with his Christian faith. And he famously succeeded!

> **FILM CLIP**
>
> In the movie. *Chariots of Fire*, Eric Liddle is the son of a Christian missionary and also happens to be the fastest sprinter in Scotland. Primed to be a major competitor at the 1922 Olympics in Paris, Liddle learns and teaches many lessons about how faith, callings, and natural abilities co-exist in his person, but not without tension. Liddle carries on a dialogue with his sister, who wants him to commit to missionary work and let go of his track commitments. Liddle concedes that he was put on this earth for a reason, but then adds a qualifier that complicates things: "God made me for a purpose, but God also made me fast! And when I run, I feel God's pleasure."[1] Well, if exercising one's ability

---

1 Hudson, *Chariots*, 1:52:05–1:56:42.

gives pleasure to God, I'm not so sure that is in any way contrary to God's purpose. Perhaps a better rendering for Liddle would be, "God made me for a purpose, *and* God also made me fast!" The 1922 Olympics became the scene for a joyous celebration of Liddle's God-given ability to run.

For someone like Eric Liddle, how could his gift of running fast be a calling? What could this gift accomplish in partnership with God?

LEARNING: CELEBRATING GOD'S INTENTIONALITY IN OUR ABILITIES

Decoding God's intentions

As Richard Bolles makes clear in the quote above, clues to God's intention for us are written into our very members and faculties in the form of natural abilities (along with our personality, values, and passions). While we may be tempted to regard abilities like carpentry as non-spiritual or unrelated to our faith, think again. Who do we think made us in the first place? And do we really think God would endow us with gifts and abilities *for no particular reason*? Unlikely. In fact, the first reason God gifted us with natural abilities is for our own pleasure. Like Eric Liddle, hopefully all of us can identify that activity in which we take great pleasure. Rest assured, we are feeling God's pleasure as we do so.

Martin Luther reminds us in his explanation of the first article of the Apostle's Creed, "I believe that God has made me and all creatures; that He has given me my body and soul, eyes, ears, and all my members, my reason and all my senses and still preserves them."[2] Luther's beautiful, earthy description of the gifts we enjoy simply as participants in creation are examples of God's gracious benevolence. We have all these things, Luther points out, without any merit or worthiness of our own. They are gifts, plain and simple—gifts that include our abilities! This very giftedness points us to the second reason God has endowed us with gifts and abilities: to equip us for our positive participation in the community of creation. Indeed, we are created out of love for love.

Equipped as you are with your faculties and abilities, it should come as no surprise, then, that what you are capable of doing is of great interest

---

2 Luther quoted in Kolb and Wengert, *Book of Concord*, 354.

to God. When the Israelites were wandering in the wilderness, they were commanded by God to construct a mobile sanctuary for worship. It fell on two individuals named Bezalel and Oholiab, who had special abilities for this. As you read this passage from Exodus, highlight in the passage your answers to two questions: first, how many different skills or jobs are mentioned? Second, how many action verbs are used to describe God's relationship with his people?

> Then Moses said to the Israelites: See, the Lord has called by name Bezalel son of Uri son of Hur, of the tribe of Judah; he has filled him with divine spirit, with skill, intelligence, and knowledge in every kind of craft, to devise artistic designs, to work in gold, silver, and bronze, in cutting stones for setting, and in carving wood, in every kind of craft. And he has inspired him to teach, both him and Oholiab son of Ahisamach, of the tribe of Dan. He has filled them with the skill to do every kind of work done by an artisan or by a designer or by an embroiderer in blue, purple, and crimson yarns, and in fine linen, or by a weaver—by any sort of artisan or skilled designer.
>
> Bezalel and Oholiab and everyone skillful to whom the Lord has given skill and understanding to know how to do any work in the construction of the sanctuary shall work in accordance with all that the Lord has commanded. (Exod 35:30—36:1).

How many different skills and jobs did you identify? How many ways does God interact with and shape the activity of God's people? It is important to note that these biblical characters all contribute their skills in a highly collaborative relationship with God. It is God who has given them their skills, both calling and inspiring them to use their skills for a worthy purpose. It would not have occurred to these Israelites that they could unilaterally decide who they choose to be in this world and what skills they would like to have. Both skills and utilization are gifts from God. But this has become confused in our day. Add each of us to a long list of people in this world who have the skills that are needed to make the world a better and more trustworthy place. Like this passage in Exodus, the God who made us is shaping and leading our lives to that end.

Barriers to embracing our natural abilities

THE MYTH OF LIMITLESSNESS AND THE IMPORTANCE OF LIMITS

The first barrier to claiming our natural abilities is the delusion of limit-lessness. As observed already, modern and postmodern Western culture has been fertile soil for various humanist fallacies, not least among them the notion that a person has no limits to what they can do and be. We are told repeatedly that you can become whatever you choose to be if you just believe in yourself. This fallacy is the logical outcome of our cosmic coup, where we gave God the boot and replaced God with, well, you and me. This little switcheroo has produced powerful delusions of grandeur wherein we think we can create our own identity, meaning, and future from scratch, ex nihilo. And yet, we are, in the end, just creatures. Creatures with big brains and considerable abilities—but finite creatures nonetheless. And I might add, creatures each with a personality and set of gifts that lend themselves to some things and not to others.

The late Don Clifton, the father of "Strengths-Based Psychology,"[3] contended that "You cannot be anything you want to be—but you can be a lot more of who you already are."[4] The development of strengths psychology has been instrumental in helping people identify their strengths and the personality that gives rise to them. Of course, finding your strengths is only the beginning. Then the challenge is to cultivate those strengths, maximize them, and find a place in this world that fits you. For the person of faith, we can take heart that our strengths—along with our personality, passions, interests, etc.—constitute how God has equipped us to play the roles we are called to play in this world. Our strengths will indelibly shape how it is that we will love others and make the world a better place.

While it seems so logical to focus on the assets we have, we also live in a world that mercilessly judges us according to what assets we don't have—how we are deficient in our personality, looks, skill sets, etc. We turn now to the very real barrier of focusing too much on our weaknesses.

STRENGTHSFINDER AND THE GAP THEORY OF CHANGE

In American culture, the default theory of self-development and change is located in deficit thinking. Focus on your weaknesses! In other words, find out what your weaknesses are and then craft a strategy to improve

---

3 Rath, *StrengthsFinder* 2.0, 1.
4 Clifton quoted in Rath, *StrengthsFinder* 2.0, 9.

on wherever you happen to be weak. This same strategy is used in organizations as they do long-range planning and attempt to become more successful. They identify the gap between where they are and where they'd like to be and then attempt to change by focusing on closing that gap. Typically, the gap is a glaring weakness, so closing it will require a steep learning curve.

Admittedly, identifying weaknesses and addressing them is not invalid in itself. In fact, it's important, for two reasons. First, we all need to become more functional in ways we currently are not. It will likely require hard work, but sometimes we just need to improve in certain areas. If you are a bad listener, it shows great wisdom to work on becoming a better one. If you have anger management issues, obviously it needs to be addressed and worked on. Addressing weaknesses that have strong implications for one's health—and the health of one's relationships—is imperative.

Second, sometimes knowing one's weaknesses—individually and corporately—means knowing when to let someone else address it! In other words, there are times when the solution to one's weakness is not to work at it personally, but to farm it out to someone else or add someone else to the team. For instance, if you know you're bad with numbers, the answer may not be trying to improve yourself in this regard, but rather letting your spouse manage the finances (of course, assuming they are better with numbers). If your team lacks members with strong people skills, you better find new team members that have effective communication skills with others. What we do with our deficiencies shows us what we do with our finitude and imperfections. Often, it's not worth it to try to become proficient with a natural deficiency when you can let someone else do it. We only have so much time and energy! This is part of accepting ourselves for who we are.

The real problem is not identifying weaknesses and accounting for them (which, again, we must do). The problem is when we make addressing our weaknesses the central strategy moving forward. This somehow presumes we need to be perfect and have no weaknesses, so we devote way too much energy to our deficiencies. To be sure, being balanced is a good thing and it is beneficial to strive for it, yet no individual—or corporate entity—can have it all. We will always be good at some things, and not so good at others. So, if you are a natural salesperson with minimal creative aptitude, why aspire to be an artist or novelist when you already have the people skills necessary for sales—such as listening, persuasion, and problem-solving? If you run a business with a track record of being cutting-edge, why try to develop a traditional product when you already have the capacity to be one step ahead?

Strengths psychology tells us to become more of what we already are. To be good at some things means you're equipped to do something particularly well. So, to put it bluntly, *do that thing!* If you invest time, resources, and energy cultivating your limited gifts, you may experience modest improvement and become functional. If you put the same resources and attention into where you are truly gifted, you can excel!

TRYING TO SATISFY WHAT OTHERS SAY YOU SHOULD BE

The third barrier is trying to justify ourselves to someone around us. Battling a culture of shame as a young monk, Luther had the burden of trying to please a demanding God and appease his guilty conscience. Interestingly, he had already failed to please his demanding father, who was very set on his son becoming a lawyer and was not impressed with Martin's decision to join the monastery. Hence, Luther had to deal with both the disappointment of his father and Luther's own perceived shortcomings in satisfying his heavenly father. Hats off to Martin Luther for not caving to what his father wanted him to do, even though it was clearly within his gift set. But Luther was also gifted to be a theological genius! Few of us struggle with justifying ourselves to God the way Luther did because we've done our best in Western culture to domesticate and tame God. But many today can certainly relate to the existential angst Luther must have felt over weighing his father's designs on his future.

In truth, the need to justify ourselves to *someone* is still there, but today it merely shifts to a different arena with different judges—the people and culture that make up the world we live in. As we feel the pressure to be what someone else wants us to be—it could be a parent or anyone we look up to—the end result can stifle our understanding of our natural abilities in order to please (or appease!) someone else. You may have even been shamed for expressing an interest in what you really feel is your God-given talent. In a world that puts so much pressure on us to distinguish ourselves, many live with the shame of not measuring up, instead dwelling on their perceived inferiority to those they think are more gifted than they are.

Once again, in this scenario, we see that part of the problem is focusing on what we lack talent-wise, as opposed to what we have. It is God's intention we understand that each of us is gifted with natural abilities that are gifts both to us and, through our agency, to our neighbor. The need to appease God or justify ourselves is, of course, a moot point. God alone saves us—not our efforts, abilities, diligence, or star power. Justified by God, we are free to let our gifts be straightforwardly life-giving to those around us. The person of faith is given an incredible gift of freedom: the freedom to be yourself and know that yourself and your abilities are good enough! God says so.

This is a most crucial point in Luther's vocational theology. Often in life, we are preoccupied with ourselves, what we are good at, how we measure up, and so on. This self-absorption, as we discussed earlier, is life turned in on itself—incurvatus se, as the church fathers taught us. Needless to say, it is very difficult to effectively love someone else when we are mostly concerned with justifying our existence, whether to God, others, or ourselves. And that is exactly how and why justification pivots into vocation. Trusting that I am justified, gifted, and have no need to prove myself, I am now free to focus entirely on the needs of my neighbor. We are freed from the task of self-justification so that we can love others and participate in community with them.

FALSE HUMILITY

Finally, I want to address an obstacle that can be significant for people of faith who value humility (as we should!). As we learn to trust that we have God-given talents (and maybe worry less about whether we are talented!), we may hesitate to celebrate those talents in any way. After all, we're supposed to be humble as Christians, right? But here we've confused humility with being talentless. With this twisted logic, identifying your talents and boldly putting them into play is not humble, but boastful. It's also a denial of God's blessings, which sometimes take the form of natural abilities! So, let's make sure we know who gets credit for our natural abilities: God. To discern what God is up to within us, it helps immensely to acknowledge that our creator has gifted us generously and for a purpose.

RESOURCES

Just as there are many resources for personality assessments, so too are there many aptitude assessments available. And quite frankly, these two categories often overlap a great deal with each other. One such assessment that I recommend, based on strengths psychology, is called

StrengthsFinder 2.0.[5] This is a short book, easy to use and aimed at helping one identify their strengths as a person—which suggests natural abilities. Interestingly, though, the StrengthsFinder assessment was originally conceived as a personality assessment. This might be because its taxonomy is all about strengths that come directly out of a handful of archetypal personalities. For most people, one of these archetypes is primary, but everyone has elements of all of them to some degree. The four archetypal personalities that delineate how people interact with others and process information are, hence, characterized by verbs in the present indicative voice: executing, influencing, relationship building, and strategic thinking. The assessment can also be taken online with many different sites, but I recommend going right to the current home of StrengthsFinder at gallup.com/cliftonstrengths. Strengthsfinder has partnered with Gallup and renamed their assessment "CliftonStrengths" (named after its founder, Don Clifton), complete with a summary and interpretation of the results.[6]

The other skills aptitude test I would like to highlight was created by American psychologist John Holland and is known as the Holland Codes or RIASEC. The Holland Codes are based on a taxonomy of six diverse clusters of natural abilities that define a certain type of person. They are: "Realistic (Doers), Investigative (Thinkers), Artistic (Creators), Social (Helpers), Enterprising (Persuaders), and Conventional (Organizers)."[7] At the website personalityjunkie.com, RIASEC is paired with MBTI, which, taken together gives a rich portrait of ones' personality, interests, and skills.[8] However, I would contend that each cluster is based on specific skills—like fix-it skills or acting ability—and is not completely dependent on one's underlying personality. For instance, someone who has "Realistic" life gifts (natural abilities) is likely mechanically inclined and a good athlete. But we also know that athletes and mechanics, for instance, can be introverted or extroverted, thinking-oriented or feeling-oriented, etc. In other words, all kinds of personalities have realistic life gifts. So, it is not accurate, in my assessment, to associate realistic life gifts with a certain personality.

---

5 Rath, *StrengthsFinder 2.0.*
6 "CliftonStrengths."
7 "Holland Code (RIASEC) Career Interests."
8 "Holland Code (RIASEC) Career Interests."

About those talents you have, biblically speaking

In Matthew 25:14–30, Jesus tells a parable about stewardship, where a man entrusts "talents," or money, to three of his servants while he is away. Two of them use their talents to double their initial amount—in one case, five talents are doubled to ten; in the other, two are doubled to four. The third servant who is only given one talent, however, hides the talent in the ground because he is afraid of his master's reaction if he were to misuse the talent. When the master returns from his trip and asks for an accounting from his servants, he is most pleased with the two who used their talents to multiply them, so he rewards them with more talents. But the master is most displeased with the servant who buried his talent in the ground. The only talent he was given is taken away and given to the servant who now has ten talents.

The point of this? We are all entrusted with gifts from God—certainly money, but also the many kinds of gifts we are exploring in this book. It can be easily summarized this way: all that you have and all that you are! And we are expected by God not only to enjoy our gifts, but also to utilize them for a bigger purpose. Co-creating with God a more trustworthy, loving, and faith-filled world.

But are the gifts we're given *really ours*? Biblical stewardship principles stress that as humans, we are taking care of God's creation—including all that we have and all that we are—as stewards, not owners. It all belongs to God and always will. In this sense, gifts are not *gifts* the way we understand them in this worldly life. They are not, technically speaking, ours. And yet there is a sense in which we're not just taking care of someone else's stuff. Our body and our faculties, our abilities and interests, our justification and salvation—our very lives—are freely given to us out of love. So, we are invited to accept our gifts with gratitude, and use them with love and creativity as if they were our own. At the same time, we understand that we ourselves and all that we have belong to Jesus. This is a qualified ownership, one might say. Often the truth is a paradox.

In the spirit of fully making use of our gifts and not hiding them away or squandering them, our gifts themselves are a summon to us! Engage with all that you have and all that you are, with thanksgiving and for the sake of your neighbor.

SUMMARY

In this chapter, we reviewed the giftedness of each one of us in the form of our natural abilities. Such abilities are not there by accident, but constitute part of what we are equipped with—clues to what God is calling us to do. A great example and metaphor are found in the story of God calling the Israelites to build a temple in the wilderness using the many gifts of craft and construction present in the people. While the purpose is determined by God, the execution is made possible by God working through the abilities of the people and shaping their work together.

We also identified obstacles present in our culture for identifying and using your gifts. We are sometimes fooled into thinking we can be anything if we put our minds to it, and yet our limits and finitude would suggest otherwise. Discern the gifts you have and go from there! We are also misled to focus on what we do not do well, as if we are supposed to become accomplished in every possible way. No, it is better to accept, once again, that we lack some abilities, and to instead focus on developing what we do have. We examined the powerful dynamic in modern life to please or appease someone (or our culture itself) by demonstrating certain gifts or being the person *they* want us to be. These are just contemporary ways that we keep chasing our own justification in the eyes of *someone*. Yet, it is God alone who justifies us freeing each of us to be who we are and use what we have been given! Finally, we live in a society that often frowns on someone acknowledging their gifts, as if that means they are full of themselves, or something similar. Pushing back on that notion, we are being bad stewards of what God has given us if we do not identify our abilities and discern how God is calling us to use them. Hiding our talents in false modesty is not helpful and not pleasing to God.

A NEW CREATION AWAITS

We have now completed Part I, entitled "Co-creating a trustworthy world with God." This, of course, is our general calling in this world, whether we perceive it or not. Often, we do not, due in no small measure to the world itself. This broken, sinful world gives us a distorted lens through which to view life and self. In our delusion, we have eaten from the proverbial apple in the garden and thereby proclaimed our independence and embraced God-like intentions. This very stumble, this curving in on self, is now embedded in the fabric of our cultures, communities, and the air we breathe. And so, we are stuck in an anthropocentric (human-centered) worldview where our gifts and opportunities are used primarily for our own agendas and advancement, as opposed to our servanthood in the community of God. We are indeed called every day to co-create a more trustworthy world with God, but as we know all too well, the world is far from trustworthy. "We confess that we are captive to sin and cannot free ourselves,"[9] reads the confession of sin in Lutheran confessional liturgy. Much earlier Paul wrote the same idea: "I can will what is right, but I cannot do it." (Rom 7:18).

"Who will free me from this body of sin that is carrying me to death? Thanks be to God through Jesus Christ our Lord!" (Rom 7:24).

Part II is God's response to our futility—becoming incarnate in human flesh in order to bear the brunt of our disease upon God's own self and die, then rise again as the beginning of a new humanity, a new creation. This new creation has been extended to us, even as we muddle through the old one. As a result, our callings expand as we witness to the new creation in Christ with the certainty that God's will for abundant life will come to fruition. That makes meaningful work even more meaningful!

Part II is entitled, "Living in the promise of the new creation in Christ."

Reflection and conversation: processing what you've learned

1. Using one of the gift assessment tools (StrengthsFinder, RIASEC) or simply by your own self-assessment, what natural abilities have you been given? Make a list of at least 3-5 abilities.

_____

_____

_____

_____

_____

---

9   ELCA, *Evangelical Lutheran Worship*, 95.

2. Do you feel your natural giftedness aligns well with your personality? How so, or not so?

_____

_____

_____

3. Which of your gifts/abilities are you using when you are at your best, when you are most truly yourself?[10]

_____

_____

_____

4. What version of yourself are you sometimes tempted to pursue that is not realistic or aligned with your gifts or personality?

_____

_____

_____

5. How are you currently using some of these abilities to help make the world a better place?

_____

_____

_____

10 Kise et. al, _Discover_, 11.

6. What abilities do you have that are underused, either for your own pleasure or for the sake of the world?

_____

_____

_____

7. What ability do you possess that God might be calling you to use to co-create a more trustworthy world with God?

_____

_____

_____

Wrap-up

What is one takeaway you have from this chapter?

_____

_____

_____

What is one question you have from this chapter?

_____

_____

_____

PART II

Living in the Promise of the
New Creation in Christ

LIVING IN THE PROMISE OF THE NEW CREATION IN CHRIST

While all human beings are called to love God and neighbor, and to seek justice, peace, and equity in our relations with others, we fail to do so consistently or without compromising motives. This is because we have failed to fear, love, and trust God. Instead, we trust in our own self-determination—the deception that we (individually and collectively) don't need God and can, therefore, function just fine as the center of our existence. But this has resulted in turning the gift of life in upon itself (incurvatus), which ultimately destroys life and allows sin and death to have the last word. In a nutshell, God's creation—and our world—is doomed. We simply do not manage our world and human community with either the requisite wisdom or goodness—even with our best intentions and efforts to let God assist us. Hence, God's Commandments remain essential as a calling to all of us to use our many gifts to help restrain sin in this broken world and protect life. That is the best we can do.

The only way we can be saved from our distorted humanity is for an antidote to be created that can destroy the disease of incurvatus, allowing creation to be reborn as a new creation. This is what Part II is about, and it means that in addition to the callings of the first creation that we've already covered, there is a new kind of calling: bearing witness to the new creation in Christ. And for this new calling, we have more gifts that have been given:

- The gift of the Holy Spirit
- The gift of being born anew into the body of Christ, the new creation
- The gift of *being* Christ in the world
- The gift of the church
- The spiritual gifts given by the Holy Spirit for the work of building up the body of Christ
- The gift of freedom that comes with the unconditional promises of God that justify us
- The gift of hope through the promised and present kingdom of God
- The gift of others with whom to converse, console, and serve

We now explore what these gifts mean both for our own abundant life and the abundant life of our neighbor. As we do so, we are encouraged by the fact that the meaningful work we've discussed in Part I—even with the cloud of sin hanging over our heads—becomes even more meaningful with the promise of the second creation. It makes a difference when you know that in the end, the values and promises you are living for will in fact come to pass. This means that every act of obedience and love in our broken world matters. A lot. We're not merely doing the right thing in a *wrong* world; we're leaning into the world to come!

Someday

Somewhere

We'll find a new way of living

We'll find a way of forgiving

Somewhere.

—*Steven Sondheim, West Side Story*

CHAPTER 7

THE HOPE AND PROMISE OF A NEW CREATION

CHAPTER OVERVIEW

In this chapter, we are introduced to the idea that everyone knows on some level that the world we now live in is not the way it *should* be—the way it's *supposed to* be. Virtually all religious and moral movements are based on that fundamental idea, which offers an insight into the way human beings are created: we can't help but look up. Christian theology holds that creation is based on God's law which expresses God's will and calling for human beings to love and trust God, love our neighbor, and care for this world. However, it is the testimony of scripture and of human history itself that this creation has been fatally distorted by human greed and folly. Things are not what they are supposed to be, and we have made it this way. But by the power of God's creative Word, a new creation (kingdom) based on God's promises will establish God's will for the future. Martin Luther spoke of these different realities as two *kingdoms*, but also as *creations*. We will use both, but primarily creations.

Both creations belong to God, and God is at work in both. Therefore, two different kinds of callings emerge from the two distinct realities in which we live. This is important because Christian callings have been colonized for too long in special churchly endeavors that amount to extraordinary pursuits added to life. As Martin Luther made clear in his vocational theology, we need to reclaim the ordinary world where we live as the arena where God is at work—by ensuring that our kids get a good education, the streets are safe, commerce is thriving, parents take time to be parents, and justice is being served. God's work is being done in the first creation by co-creating with us a more trustworthy, loving, and faithful world where there is often none of those things! This is the calling of all humans, regardless of belief.

It is the unique calling of the Christian, however, to bear witness to the unconditional promise of God that in Christ is a new creation. Therefore, we simultaneously proclaim and embody (however imperfectly) the values of the new creation while immersing ourselves purposefully in the old creation. This is nothing short of a rebirth.

Introduction to the hope and promise of a new creation

FILM CLIP

In the movie, *The Mission*, we find an excellent illustration of humans twisting creation to serve their purposes. We encounter the real world of eighteenth-century colonialism in South America. The Portuguese at that time practiced human trafficking. They were ready to harvest an indigenous village where a Jesuit mission was working peacefully with the native peoples. The Jesuits pleaded with the political powers to leave their peaceful mission alone. However, the desire and profitability of owning people were too strong. At one point, the already deeply complicit Cardinal Altamirano is being persuaded to let the trafficking continue, even disrupting the missions sent by God. Says one official, "We must work in the world, your eminence. The world is thus." Altamirano replies, "No, Senor Hontar. Thus, we have made the world ... thus I have made it."[1] Now there's a confession. This is also the reason the Ten Commandments were given.

---

1 Joffé, *The Mission*, 1:57:40—1:59:02.

LEARNING: PLAYING OUT OF POSITION IN THE FIRST CREATION

It says in Gen 2:15 that we were created to be partners with God and "to till and keep the garden," which means to till and keep *creation*. We were called to be gardeners, to protect and nurture God's Garden of life. In all these scenarios, God is the owner whose purpose is being served, namely, the flourishing of life for all.

However, as we learned with the tree of the knowledge of good and evil, we humans often prefer to *be* God—to be the owners. God also told the people he had created that they were to have "dominion" (Gen 1:28) over God's creation and its creatures. The correct meaning of the word dominion in its original sense was very close to the contemporary meaning of the word stewardship, which means to care for and nurture life—as a gardener would do—in alignment with the owner's purposes.[2] What dominion does not mean here is *to dominate* or *exploit*. What humans have done throughout history, however, is interpret dominion as precisely that, namely, as domination. In other words, to use the natural world (and each other) for one's own purposes rather than the owner's. This is what happened when the humans God created ate from the tree of the knowledge of good and evil. They were declaring that they didn't trust God and rather wished to be in control, independent of God. Theologian Douglas John Hall has pointed out, though, that as the ones in control of creation, we humans are neither wise enough nor good enough on our own to be in charge.[3] We are creatures made to be dependent on our creator's moral vision and agency. And now, operating from a human-centered perspective, we are playing out of position, as they might say in the sports world.

And now our relationship with God and our trust in God is broken. Our human nature is distorted, and that distortion is extended to creation itself. We turn away from loving our neighbor as a *subject* and turn to using our neighbor as an *object* to serve our agendas. It is within this context that the Ten Commandments were given as a gift to the Israelites. God was trying to help them return to God and turn positively toward their neighbors by recapturing their roles as gardeners and stewards. And so, the Ten Commandments are a restraining order, given to restrain sin and protect us from each other. They are also, as we have seen, exhortations to *proactively* love our neighbor and God. But one of the most overlooked functions of God's law is to keep us humble by showing us that we ultimately fail to do what God's law requires of us, namely, to love and trust

---

2 Fretheim, *Interpreters Bible*, 39.
3 Hall, *Darkness*, 165.

God and love our neighbor. The Ten Commandments, then, make the case for an intervention by God to reboot humanity, and creation. Since the Commandments are written on every person's heart and, for the most part, are stated one way or another in all the major religions, they do indeed tell us that something is wrong. They are a mirror in which we see who we really are.

The second creation: getting re-connected to God

Lutheran theologian Carl Braaten writes that there is a universal split in the human condition between our awareness of the way things are and what they ought to be.[4] Even non-believers testify to this split between what *is* and what *ought to be* in their assumptions and actions. Simply put, we know there is a better world out there somewhere. This awareness shows itself in three ways. First, human beings seem to have an almost universal and powerful intuition that the end of our earthly existence is not the end, but that there's something more. Indeed, it is common to hear someone say that so-and-so, who has died, is looking down on us now from another reality. And so-and-so is often not a religious person. Second, common human experience testifies to a moral and spiritual intuition that tells us the compromised, broken world we live in is not supposed to be this way. This only makes sense if there is supposed to be another way, a different way, that reflects a just and life-giving realm where all enjoy abundant life. Third, we observe within the human race (admittedly, some more than others) the relentless drive to make changes in this world through education and social reform because, again, we instinctively know there's a better way and a better world waiting for us to claim. Knowing something is seriously wrong with our world, we all long for salvation. This is our entry point into the second creation. Few times has this point been made as poignantly as it was in a popular stage and movie production we know well.

FILM CLIP

In the movie, *West Side Story*, the love Tony and Maria feel for each other is doomed by the unforgiving, tribal world in which they live. Sensing this doom closing in around them, they imagine and desperately cling to the belief in a world somewhere, where people will learn "a new way of living," and "find a way of forgiving." As they sing the iconic song, *Somewhere*, it is clear that on some level, they do indeed believe it! [5]

---

4 Braaten, *Principles*, 65-67.
5 Robbins and Wise, *West Side Story*, 1:47:30–1:51:06.

"Somewhere" according to scripture

West Side Story illustrates this very longing for salvation and the anticipation of a place where we have not yet arrived. In his writings, Braaten reminds us of the source of salvation: "There is no world from which God is absent and in which he does not stir up a longing for salvation which he alone can bring."[6] Christians believe that *that* salvation is a new creation promised to us by God and, in fact, already begun in Jesus Christ. This new creation fulfills God's intentions for humankind as well as humankind's yearning for itself. This creation is anchored in a renewed relationship with God and is based on God's unconditional promise, not God's law. It's not the law, but a relationship with God that will give us new life.

Much of the Bible describes a grand reboot, a salvation that God alone can bring. This is described frequently in prophecies and it is a promise. For example, in Revelation we read a vivid description of a new creation when God will wipe away every tear!

Then I saw a new heaven and a new earth … "See, the home of God is among mortals. He will dwell with them as their God; they will be his peoples, and God himself will be with them; he will wipe every tear from their eyes. Death will be no more; mourning and crying and pain will be no more, for the first things have passed away" (Rev 21:1–4).

Or in Isaiah, when God promises that one day people will be at peace with one another.

> He shall judge between the nations and shall arbitrate for many peoples; they shall beat their swords into plowshares, and their spears into pruning hooks; nation shall not lift up sword against nation, neither shall they learn war anymore (Isa 2:4).

In the New Testament, the central theme is the fulfillment of prophecies in the person of Jesus of Nazareth. The following verse from Luke 4:18–21 records Jesus's first public reading and statement. He announces that he has fulfilled a prophecy from Isaiah. Fulfillment guarantees the outcome, but it is not the same as fruition. Fruition is the full realization of an outcome that has not yet arrived. Not even close.

---

6 Braaten, *Principles*, 65-67.

> The Spirit of the Lord is upon me because he has anointed me to bring good news to the poor. He has sent me to proclaim release to the captives and recovery of sight to the blind, to let the oppressed go free, to proclaim the year of the Lord's favor ... Today this scripture has been fulfilled in your hearing.

Elsewhere, it is said in the New Testament that Christ is the firstborn of a new humanity that fulfills God's intentions for us and restores a right relationship of faith and trust between humankind and God (Col 1:15–20). Baptism is our birth into the new humanity established by Christ, a new creation where we are liberated from sin and death. Baptism is also the death of the old self. But just as we don't yet fully experience the liberation of the new self, we don't leave our old self behind just yet. The outcome for us is guaranteed by God, even though the new and old creations are always in tension in and around us. In this life, we live with one foot in each creation. Paul expresses this dual movement.

> Do you not know that all of us who have been baptized into Christ Jesus were baptized into his death? Therefore, we have been buried with him by baptism into death, so that, just as Christ was raised from the dead by the glory of the Father, so we too might walk in newness of life. For if we have been united with him in a death like his, we will certainly be united with him in a resurrection like his (Rom 6:3–5).

It must be stressed that the gift of a new creation is the gift of God to us in an incomprehensible act of reckless love. That God would create again using God's *own blood* and solidarity with humanity is a gift unlike any other. The gift of God's own self in Jesus Christ opens up a plethora of new gifts that emanate from God's unconditional promise of new life. Those gifts, of course, flow to us and *through* us to our neighbors. In the chapters ahead, we will unpack those gifts and callings that result from participating in the new creation of which Jesus was the firstborn. The callings issuing from within the second and new creation are summed by one word: *witness*. Yes, we continue to love our neighbor in all the dimensions of this earthly life, and indeed we do so with God. But now God, through Christ, has made us participants in a new realm that is based entirely on the promises of God. This is a message that must be spoken, shown, pointed to, and embodied in any way possible. And as I've already alluded to, the meaning of our acts of love and obedience to God's law is enhanced greatly by the fact that the new creation will transform the old; God's kingdom will come to us.

SUMMARY

We have observed that the world in which we live and work—and engage our callings with our many gifts!—is stuck in a devastating anthropocentrism from which we cannot rise up. Again, the words of our confessional liturgy: "We confess that we are captive to sin and cannot free ourselves."[7] Much of our experience in our callings is to restrain sin and protect life as we work with God to more fully establish a trustworthy world. None of this is to say that we are incapable of experiencing joy, hope, and love in this world, and yet we are painfully aware that this world we live in is deeply broken. It is not the way the world should be. Somehow, we are aware, deep down, that there is another world that represents the values that we know are right and good, but so often unattainable to us. As *West Side Story* reminds us in a hopeful lament, "Somewhere, we'll find a new way of living … a way of forgiving."[8]

This powerful intuition in human experience points directly to the very center of the Christian faith, namely, that in Christ God has chosen solidarity with us in our brokenness, taken its weight upon his shoulders, and through Christ raised a new creation that has defeated sin and death. This is our salvation, that our trust is restored in the God of life and that we are created anew. Our faith is also our calling: to bear witness to this new creation based on the presence and promises of God where human life and human community become whole. Coming back to our initial existential question about meaning, we now know that meaning is deepened and enriched because we are not fighting a losing battle. God's intentions of abundant life for us will come to pass!

---

7   ELCA, *Evangelical Lutheran Worship*, 95.
8   Robbins and Wise, *West Side Story*, 1:47:30—1:51:06.

Reflection and conversation: processing what you've learned

1. What have you learned about the first creation? What have you learned about the second creation?

_____

_____

_____

2. In God's first creation, God and God's expectations are available to all. Again, these are given in creation as a part of the universal church. What does it mean for us that our neighbor of a different faith also has a relationship with God and knows what is right? How might we find common ground with them and work together?

_____

_____

_____

3. As we consider the second creation, when and where do you find yourself longing for _somewhere_? What does it look like for you when you imagine the fulfillment of life, when reconciliation is complete?

_____

_____

_____

4. Christian theology insists that the human race and the world we have distorted through our broken trust in God cannot be turned around by human initiative, but must be saved by God. What has the word "saved" come to mean in popular culture?

_____

_____

_____

5. How do you react to the idea that God in Christ has done a re-boot—a _do-over_, if you will—with creation?

_____

_____

_____

6. What might this new creation mean for your life? For your callings?

_____

_____

_____

7. Put together a description of what the second creation is. Remember, the second creation is based on God's promises and intentions for what human life looks like. What are its values? What are its characteristics? As Christians, the second creation should be as vivid to us as the first creation.

_____

_____

_____

8. What would it be like to be *fully human again* by being content to be creatures who are in a dependent, trusting relationship with God?

_____

_____

_____

Wrap-up

What questions do you have as we end this chapter?

_____

_____

_____

Takeaways?

_____

_____

_____

A Christian lives in Christ through faith,
in the neighbor through love.

—*Martin Luther, The Freedom of a Christian*

CHAPTER 8

THE GIFT OF A NEW SELF

Review and reflection

We have just made the pivot from the first creation—in which we live—to the new creation that is revealed in Christ. Just as we continue to love our neighbor and partner with God to co-create a more trustworthy world, we now bear witness to God's victory at the conclusion of human history—a victory which is already present and alive in Jesus Christ. Because God has created a new humanity through Jesus of Nazareth, we know that our trust in God can be restored, that love will win, and abundant life will be established for all. What does it mean to take on the callings that issue forth as members of the new creation, the body of Christ? How do we witness to this transformative reality? This is the task at hand: to explore the callings of one who is baptized into the body of Christ.

CHAPTER OVERVIEW

In this chapter, I will introduce participants to the idea that just as we live in a fallen world, through baptism we are also simultaneously part of a new creation in Christ, which will one day transform the creation we know all too well. The new creation is both gift and calling to us. It is made possible by the life, death, and resurrection of Jesus Christ and the power of the Holy Spirit. We will also explore the flip side of baptism: death. Just as we are born into a new creation by the waters of baptism, those same waters are also at work destroying our old self that is yoked to this fallen world.

Our baptism into the body of Christ is best understood through Luther's favorite metaphor to describe how it is that Christ saves us, namely, the "joyful exchange."[1] In this exchange, Christ takes on our sin, brokenness, and death, bearing it for us and with us so that it will not destroy us. From Christ we receive—as our own—the righteousness, abundant life, and community of God. We belong to Christ, who has given us everything! We are Christ's. In fact, the joyful exchange of our baptism in Christ is our first calling: as Luther expressed in the Small Catechism, the Holy Spirit has called us through the gospel promise to *be* a new creation in Christ, to live in Christ through the gift of faith. Our calling is to be a member of the body of Christ and to participate in the perichoretic (triune God as dynamic community) dance—a dance that begins with the body of believers we experience in a congregation, but extends further to our neighbors in the world.

Here we move on to callings that directly follow the contours of the double movement of the joyful exchange. As beneficiaries of this exchange with Christ, we also transition to a new way of being. Participating directly in the life, community, and love of God, *we are now Christs* for the world. That is, in our very being we reprise the twofold drama of the joyful exchange, living in love for our neighbor. So, just as Christ has borne our burdens, brokenness, and frailties as his own in the first movement of the exchange, we, too, are called to be Christ to our neighbor for our neighbor's sake, to help them bear their burdens and let them know they are not alone. Not alone indeed! In the second movement of the joyful exchange, *we are Christs* to our neighbor as we convey the message—however we can—that God has promised to make his goodness, life, and community their own as well! And so, "We are Christ's—with and without the apostrophe."

The strength of this declaration that *we are Christ* is, of course, not our own faith and strength but the presence of God in, with, and under us. Any one of us, even as we live the joyful exchange, will often struggle with the emptiness of our fallen humanity. Regardless, God will work through us even when we are generally unreceptive. Furthermore, often we will

---

1 Simpson, "No Trinity," 271.

find that it is our neighbor who bears the life-giving presence of Christ for us, for God is at work in them, too.

While we live in both creations, it is the new creation in Christ that has created the church and led to the pouring out of the Holy Spirit in the church's life. We now turn to what it means to be called by a God who has recreated us, just as we continue to live in a world that is broken. As a new creation, we have now moved way beyond what it means to volunteer at church. Indeed, we *are* the church, for we are the body of Christ. Let's compare our baptismal calling with our understanding of volunteering at church (or anywhere).

Introduction to baptism as a calling

VOLUNTEERING IN THE CHURCH
What is your experience volunteering at church? What is the most positive experience you've had volunteering at church?

_____

_____

_____

Have you ever considered that volunteering is a part of your baptism? If so, how?

_____

_____

_____

Do you ever feel that you don't have time to volunteer, that you can barely get through your regular schedule?

_____

_____

_____

What if you volunteered for every waking minute? How would that make you feel?

_____

_____

_____

If you volunteered for every waking minute, you'd have to completely give up your life! That wouldn't even be volunteering anymore. It would simply be _who you are_. In baptism, we die and rise, and that is who we are, 24/7. Baptism moves us beyond volunteering. It is the genesis of a new kind of calling: callings born out of a new creation.

LEARNING: BAPTISM IS BOTH GIFT AND CALLING

ICY BAPTISM

When my friend Terry was 22, he fell through the ice on a lake near his home in Aitkin, Minnesota. He went completely down to the bottom and had the vivid experience of seeing his life flash before his eyes. He recounts seeing in great detail episodes from his childhood and youth. He saw his mom, dad, brother, and dear friends. He was aware of the situation he was in and thought he was going to die. And yet, it was also a fantastic experience; he felt at peace.

He then heard a voice asking whether he wanted to go back—go back, that is, to the world he knew. It was clear that he could stay in the water and join the next world (a wonderful place, he was quite sure).

Then Terry was called. He was suddenly seized with the revelation that he had a purpose in this life and that this was not his time. There was this sense that he could be a positive influence on the lives of others if he returned to the earthly world. Then suddenly, through no effort of his own, he found himself on the surface of the lake crawling onto the ice and off the lake. He stresses that he had no agency in ascending to the surface—or consciousness—but was _delivered_ to the surface by a power beyond his control. When he was in the water, he was close to death, and in truth, part of him died. That part of Terry did not fully realize what a gift life was, what life was for. And then he was born again. Terry is one of the most generous and thoughtful people I know. He has lived his life very much as though he had a life-and-death baptismal experience in which he was sent back into the world for a purpose.

Baptism is, in truth, *death and life*. It is putting to death the old self in us as spiritual descendants of Adam and Eve, hell-bent on being our own god, trusting in our ingenuity, falling back on the crutches and addictions of our choosing, and crafting a life designed to serve our needs. Baptism reminds us always why we were created in the first place: to be loved and to love. We were created by love for love, to celebrate the gift of life, and to help life flourish in our neighbor. In the first creation, we were made in the *image* of God, but we traded that image for our own reflection! In the second creation, we are born into the *embodiment* of God in Jesus. Big difference, between image and embodiment. It is who we are, and it means we have a new mission.

Baptism in Luther's time: shipwreck or sea-worthy?

You may recall from Part I that the Christian world of Luther's time was defined by Roman Catholicism. Catholic theology viewed the human person as broken and sinful. However, with the help of God, they could become righteous and acceptable to God. And one needed to do just that, for one could not be acceptable to God in heaven unless they had become righteous in their very person. This was achieved (or so it was thought) by a lifetime of cooperating with God, earning merit, and living up to your God-given potential.

The problem with this theology, as Luther experienced firsthand, was quite simple. If my salvation depends in part on me, how do I ever know if I've done enough? How do I know whether I've actualized my potential to an acceptable degree or instead have been fatally compromised by impure motives and lackluster follow-through? Without this assurance, I am left preoccupied with myself, counting merit, and speculating on point totals. It's a bit harder to care about your neighbor when your very fate is teetering upon your own shaky performance. In this scenario, what you really care about isn't your neighbor, but your own status.

Luther's insight was that our hope and salvation are to be found utterly and completely in God, not within ourselves. Only God can be trusted to deliver authentic goodness and righteousness. And God's promise is that God does just that! God, in Jesus, has poured out God's righteousness to us as a gift, no strings attached. Since God has met all conditions, there are none that remain for us. For us, this is an unconditional promise. Count on it! To trust in such a promise is to be saved. God's righteousness saves us, not our own. That is solely where our hope lies.

The Roman view of baptism reflected their theology of climbing upward to respectability.[2] Baptism was the first sacrament in a Christian's life, where God initially gives us the grace needed to help remake us into a righteous person. However, this grace—in the form of baptism—will only get you so far in this world. Baptism, in this theology, was like a brand-new ship in which to begin the voyage of life, carrying you through the dangerous waters of a sinful and broken world. But the turbulent waters and rocky shoals of this world will sooner or later render the good ship baptism a shipwreck. This shipwreck will be early in life, so something else will need to take over for the promise and grace of baptism, which has now run its course. Here is where the other sacraments come in. As the desperate and vulnerable believer is still clinging to the shattered timber from the destroyed baptism ship, it is time to begin going to confession and mass regularly, so that the baptized person can start receiving regular doses of God's grace and begin elevating oneself to higher ground.

Soon after will come confirmation, marriage, and, eventually, the last rites. All of this was part of God's plan, it was believed, to deliver enough grace to us as Christians, so we could elevate ourselves on the ladder of righteousness by a combination of God's grace and our own good works.

Luther's twist on this whole thing was to declare that if baptism is a ship that signifies passage to a new creation and self, it is therefore a ship that does not fall apart in this world's seas and tempests.[3] The gift and promise of our baptism is a ship that is created out of the promises of God that no rocks or storms from this world can destroy. That is because Jesus has already won—already defeated sin, death, and the devil. Our baptism into the body of Christ is something we can always count on. Baptism was and is God's act of rebirthing a broken sinner as a new creation and member of God's family. Hence, it is important to affirm our baptism every day. Here is one ship that is not going down!

So, which system do you choose—Roman or Lutheran? Where do you place your trust? In your own ability to create a certain level of righteousness in yourself, or in God's promise through baptism that you are already a part of a new creation? You are called to faith in God's promise

2 Gritsch and Jenson, *Lutheranism*, 36-40
3 Bayer, *Luther's Theology*, 268-69.

of a new creation! This is what we call pure gift—and nothing in this world can take it away.

Baptism is a matter of life and death

In Romans 6:1-11, we learn that those of us baptized into Christ Jesus—and therefore, his resurrection and eternal life—are also baptized into Jesus' death. It is a surprise to many that baptism is as much about death as it is about life. This is because the legacy left to us by the first creation is broken and distorted. Each of us is a part of this creation and a reflection of it. Therefore, we are broken and distorted. Just as water destroys life, so too does God's baptismal promise destroy the old person that we all are, hopelessly mired in a fallen world. Yet this promise is far from fully realized in us, for we all know that the old self still stubbornly clings to us and will throughout this life. Luther famously said that in the waters of baptism—which eventually drown the old self—we learn that the old self is a good swimmer. So, this will take some time. It is for this reason that the Apostle Paul writes, "I can will what is right, but I cannot do it. For I do not do the good I want, but the evil I do not want is what I do. Now if I do what I do not want, it is no longer I that do it, but sin which dwells within me" (Rom 7:18-20). So, in baptism, we are reborn in the body of Christ, a new humanity.

As indicated, we can visualize baptism as a ship that always remains seaworthy in life's waters. We might also think of baptism as the gift of a fully formed new self in a struggle with our old self (that swims well and hangs on). Because our faith is often weak and we are compromised by the world and our old self, there are many things that obscure the full expression of the new self. And thus, we remain in sin.

> ### FILM CLIP
>
> In the movie, *Tender Mercies*, a washed-up country singer who is down on his luck and struggling to stop drinking meets a woman who redeems his life with love and purpose. Her son is also a lifeline to this man. As he realizes that blessings have come his way from God, he is moved to be baptized at the local church, along with the son of his girlfriend. Afterward, they both process what just happened. They conclude that they don't feel any different … yet. This little scene is a testament to the tension

between the promise of what *will be*, and the current world and self that *is*—not yet.[4]

How then do we live with the new and the old together? That is our first and most important calling. As God through the Holy Spirit first called us to himself in faith, we have an ongoing call to be an active part of the body of Christ and nourish the new creation that we are.

The first baptismal calling: we are Christ's

In baptism we are given our first and most important calling: to the body of Christ to which we belong. The body is the community of baptized believers and the new identity each is given, born anew in Christ, who is the first fruit of the new creation. Luther and the reformers called this our general calling. It means that we, along with many others, *are Christ's*; that through faith we belong to Jesus and the whole community of God—the Perichoresis—that God has extended to all members of the fallen humanity. Its heartbeat is the dynamic inter-relationship between the Father, Son, and Holy Spirit. Our general calling is to participate in this perichoretic community and be nourished by it; to remember who we are and *whose* we are. We are nothing less than a new humanity gathered at the foot of the cross—a community that will always surprise us with its breadth and reach.

At this point, it is imperative to stress that as baptized members of the body of Christ, both the church and our faith are formed and sustained by the ongoing Word that God speaks to us. Luther referred to this as "passive righteousness,"[5] simply receiving the grace of God's constituting Word as a gift through no effort of our own. Worship, meditation, devotional times, communion, and small groups are events where passive righteousness can be practiced. This righteousness, received passively as pure gift, then becomes the very fountain for our "active righteousness."[6] Active righteousness is when we get busy with our gifts and callings and join God in the missio Dei. Indeed, the fountain of grace Luther called passive righteousness is so critical because the old self (that does not belong to Jesus) is a good swimmer and hangs on in this life much more than we would like. In short, we need to *receive* a righteousness that is more powerful than anything we can muster on our own! And, in fact, we are called to receive it.

---

4 Beresford, *Tender Mercies*, 1:04:07–1:06:08.
5 Kolb, *Genius*, 50.
6 Kolb, *Genius*, 50.

Hence, Luther taught the importance of the daily affirmation of our baptism in our lives. The old self draws us away from the body of Christ and its community, pulling us down into narcissistic and self-serving behavior. And so, as we live in the waters of our baptism, the Holy Spirit is at work, daily drowning the old self. Again, here is the violent image reminding us that the waters of baptism destroy life. But at the same time, these waters bring forth and nourish life—a new life in Christ. And this is a calling, a calling to be made anew. The Holy Spirit calls and empowers us to participate in this new creation, which is both me as an individual and the community of which we are a part. Only the Holy Spirit can equip us with the faith necessary to be a baptized believer.

Let me share a quick word with those who may feel that this Christian teaching—the drowning of our old self—may seem like self-loathing. On the contrary, this is not an exercise in self-hatred, but rather an affirmation of our best and true self. To recognize baptism as death and new life is to acknowledge that the blessing of the gift of our humanity as *imago Dei* has become distorted by incurvatus, sin. That expression of our humanity only thwarts life, and hence, must die for us to be saved. Nonetheless, we hold this self of ours tenderly and with the forgiveness that God has granted to us, for this self, distorted as it is, is our companion in this life and the very seedbed of the new creation in Christ. In the meantime, we know that in Christ our old self will not win the day, and therefore we can adopt both a confidence about a future in God's hands and a realism about the prospects for this life.

One of the major questions for each baptized Christian is how one responds to God's call to them to participate in the Holy Spirit's work of drowning the old self and bringing forth new life. For Luther, daily confession was a critical piece. Confession as a practice has fallen out of favor with most Lutherans, but that is a shame. Luther felt strongly that we needed assurance each day of God's gracious will, which forgives us, loves us, and claims us, so that we might be free. This practice can easily be incorporated into a daily devotional time of dwelling in the Word, prayer, and confession.

Also, we affirm our baptism and nourish our new self in Christ by sharing in the Lord's Supper regularly. For Luther, communion was vital for nourishing our new humanity in Christ for the daily journey in life. It is also worth pointing out that in neither sacrament are we positioned as the center of our own existence. Christ is at the center, and we are given the gift of participating in the life of God. In baptism, we die and rise again. In the Lord's Supper, we are fed for the journey of faith. Sacraments are indeed a gift and a calling. More broadly, worshipping with other members of the body of Christ is also a calling as we gather each week to remember and rehearse our story.

The calling of worship in the body of Christ has two dimensions: private and corporate. First, it is private in the sense that each of us has the calling to let the Holy Spirit go to work on us as individuals. But second, we are called to participate in the body of Christ as a community of believers to build up the body of Christ. Therefore, just as we worship and commune because we need to do this individually, so too do we also worship and commune because our fellow members of the body of Christ need us there. It is your own presence as you greet your neighbor with the peace of Christ and your presence as you sing and commune next to someone that may be an encouragement to them in ways you do not see. And the converse is true as well: we need the others in our faith community! This is the dance of Perichoresis, a way of being in community that is grounded in God's own community.

Another aspect of our calling to the body of Christ is found in gathering with other Christians for the mutual conversation and consolation of the saints, as we discussed earlier. This is essentially the description of a Christian small group, where members gather to work out faith and life together. In this conversation of the saints, we learn how to reflect and then discern God among us, encouraging one another along the way. We gather because we need it and because our brother and sister in Christ need it as well. Interestingly, Luther was close to declaring this form of gathering a sacrament, for God promised to be present where two or more are gathered (Matt 18:20). Perichoresis!

The missional church has taught us that when we practice Christian community through mutual conversation, we acquire the skills to practice community with our neighbors outside the church. More on that later.

The second calling of baptism: we are *Christs*, part I

Now we examine the pivot to our neighbor. As Christ has borne our burdens so they will not crush us, we now are called to be Christs to our neighbor, helping them bear their burdens so those burdens don't crush them. Since we belong to Christ as members of Christ's body, we have been set free from all the things that diminish and destroy life. In God's joyful exchange with us, Christ bears our brokenness for us and with us, in exchange for the gift of God's forgiveness and participation in the life of God through the perichoretic community. Hence, we have been set free from our self-justifying ways, our guilt, and our various forms of angst and narcissism that hinder us from loving our neighbor. This liberation is what drives the pivot to our neighbor, namely, that in the new creation we have been freed to love. Declared righteous with the righteousness of Christ, recreated with the life of Christ, infused with the love of Christ, and anchored by the community of the triune God, we are freed to be like Christ. Specifically, we are free to take the form of a servant—as Christ did—and to be *Christs* to our neighbor. We love our neighbor, then, for the simple reason that our neighbor needs it, not because we need to justify ourselves or merit more grace. We love with the love of Christ so that our neighbor's life might thrive. This calling to love in turn results in many different callings for each of us, each one particular to our unique identity.

Baptism is a commission to us as the priesthood of all believers to be sent back into the world to love our neighbor as ourselves and to obey the Commandments. But we are not only free to love our neighbor, we are *empowered to love our neighbor!* Because of our new relationship with God that is characterized by faith and signified by baptism, by the power of the Holy Spirit Christ is at work *in* and *through* you. Hence, through our restored relationship with God in Christ, it is not our own capacity to love upon which we are leaning, but the love from Christ (again, in this respect we are passive). Therefore, just as we trust the righteousness of Christ to justify and save us as individuals, we are also called to trust in the love and righteousness of Christ to flow through us to our neighbor. It is for this reason that Luther wrote that faith is naturally active, always looking for good works to do. Before the need can be identified, faith has already responded (now we are active!). "Oh, it is a living, busy, mighty thing this faith. It is impossible for it not to be doing good works incessantly,"[7] wrote Luther on what faith means for loving our neighbor. It turns out it means a lot.

Since we are Christs, the central core of our solidarity and presence with our neighbor is not just that *I am with you*, but that *Christ is with you!* And so, in the joyful exchange, God assumes our neighbor's burden but will do so in a partnership with me—one whose burdens are also being carried by Christ.

There is an appropriate caution here, however. This formulation of our calling to be Christ has limits. For starters, we are finite, and hence possess only so much time and energy. That means we cannot pretend

---

7   Luther qtd. in Bayer, *Luther's Theology*, 287.

to carry everyone's burdens with them. There's not enough of us to go around! So, we need to be realistic, prioritize, and listen to whom God is calling us to invest more time and energy. Failure to do so will result in unavoidable—but unnecessary—guilt. And, of course, when we are honest with ourselves, much of the time we don't feel the kind of faith Luther describes—the busy, living, mighty thing that does good works incessantly. So, let's face it: at the end of the day, we all need the grace of knowing that we will often stumble in our callings. Does that mean our faith is insufficient or that Christ does not live in us? No, to both. Remember the discussion about the co-existence of the old and new self? Your old self is a good swimmer and not easily drowned. Our old selves still live in us, and the old self gets cranky and tired. Hence, sometimes we would rather not be concerned with the needs of our neighbor or family member. That's why it's essential to remember that our callings are always compromised by the old self, the fallen world. And so, our callings are often experienced as duty: you do something because you're called to, because it is what love requires, not because you always feel like it. It is not a trivial thing that oftentimes doing the right thing, the loving thing, is our cross to bear, and it's literally killing us.

The third calling of baptism: we are *Christs*, Part II

Let's unpack some more what it means that we are Christs. In our joyful exchange with Christ, Christ takes on our brokenness as his own, while at the same time conferring to us what belongs to Christ: participation in the goodness, life, and community of God. This truth now shapes and sharpens our calling to our neighbor, for we offer the same good news to them—the good news that gives life! Our baptism as a calling means that just as Christ has forgiven our sins and promised to free us from all forms of bondage and brokenness, so, too, are we called to extend this good news to our neighbor. To review, this means we are not only called to belong to the body of Christ and to be Christs in acts of love for our neighbor. We are also called to share with them the good news of the second part of the joyful exchange: That God shares God's life, love, righteousness, and perichoretic community with them (just as God did with you and me). This is the unconditional promise of God in Christ through which our neighbor is a new creation.

We cannot leave this part out. However, it is common in many Christian circles (certainly among Lutherans) to restrict our calling as followers of Jesus to acts of love, advocacy, and solidarity. And surely this is an essential part of our everyday calling! Such actions are a major part of what it means to be Christs. But often, that's as far as it goes. Don't preach about Jesus, the thinking goes. After all, we don't want to sound like pushy evangelists. Besides, everyone has their own beliefs, so it's best to leave them alone. Or something like that.

And yet to omit conversation or proclamation about the very center of the Christian witness is a huge problem. As much as acts of love and kindness are critically important, they also do not set Christians apart from most world religions or even humanist thinking. That's well and good, for that means we have much common ground to explore here with our diverse neighbors. As Christians, we are a people who follow the God we believe became human, died, rose again, and forged a new creation that frees us from sin and death, leading to abundant life. That is a remarkable declaration! This is the sort of message that ought to be shared—assuming we believe it and do love our neighbor. None of this presumes any disrespect for what others already believe. We're just adding to the conversation when the time is right. When we are *called to listen and speak*.

And so, we are called to bear witness to the promise that true life is a pure gift; that Christ has redeemed our neighbor in a new creation—a creation where sin is forgiven, where we all belong, and where shame and grief are no more. We speak openly, unapologetically, of God's promises and the kingdom of God which is at hand in Christ. It means nothing less for me—*and my neighbor*—than God choosing to include us in the eternal perichoretic dance of life! Our neighbor will never have to be alone, without hope, or love. None of us will face death as the final act.

This is not something to keep quiet about. How do we learn to talk about such things with our neighbors? Or even with our fellow church members?

WHEN CHRIST COMES TO US THROUGH OUR NEIGHBOR

There is a danger in a pithy phrase like *We are Christs—with and without the apostrophe*. The danger is when we who are beneficiaries of the joyful exchange come to believe that we are the very ones who bring God to a world where God is not present. Instead, as I have been emphasizing in this book, we learn over and again in scripture that the triune God is loose in the world! God is present in those we least expect, in ways we might not have imagined. We do indeed bear Christ to the world around us, and indeed, the world—through our neighbors—bears Christ to us as well. And that is a good thing, for we are called to be Christ to our neighbor not only because our neighbor needs it, but because we need it!

We are members of a new humanity gathering at the foot of the cross, and we never know whose hearts have been opened to participate in this new creation. We all need to experience God's mystery and grace—some days very much so!—and this will happen not only through Word and sacrament but through others. Certainly, God comes to us through others in Christian fellowship and the universal church, which encompasses many religions. But even more than that, God comes to us in grace, love—and sometimes prodding—through others in the world at large. Luke 10 reminds us that the harvest of folks resonant with God's presence—or ready to hear the good news of Jesus—is plentiful. God is present and at work already. We will explore this theme much more in the next chapter, but it is critical to introduce it here.

IN CONCLUSION

Often, we speak in the church of volunteering and confuse this with a calling. But if our baptism is a calling to be both a part of the body of Christ and also to be in the world, then it's an all-consuming thing. If it is true that we are *Christ's* and we are *Christs*, this is our whole life. All of it. That being the case, how we make a living is as much a Christian calling as our unpaid church callings, our volunteering.

But the biggest difference between volunteering and being called is this: For the volunteer, the self is often at the center. I step up and I do what needs to be done, thereby allowing myself a (false)measure of heroism. Then I retreat to my own world again. For the baptized, God is at the center. It's about the body of Christ. God is the one who acts in and through us. We only participate. And yet, we *get to* participate. We are *called* to participate. Thanks be to God!

SUMMARY

We have examined what it means to be baptized into the body of Christ, and how this baptism is a calling. First of all, our baptism is both a death and a birth. The waters of baptism drown our sinful self that this fallen world has distorted—the first creation. Yet, baptism is also the birth of a new self into the new creation of which Jesus Christ is the beginning. Since our old self stays with us as long as we are in this world, our new self exists alongside our old self as a promise and proclamation, not a fully realized reality. While the old self hangs on in this life, it never nullifies the truth of the new life that baptism signifies. The new life we can confidently claim is the life we are living into.

Second, baptism is also a *calling*. A famous Luther quote captures the best way to understand what it means: *We are Christ's—with and without the apostrophe*. With the apostrophe, we have the possessive voice: we belong to Christ and therefore enjoy all Christ's benefits. Belonging to Christ means the life of God, Christ's righteousness, and the community of the triune God, has all been extended to me. I am called to participate in this new creation and its fellowship as one who has been redeemed and welcomed into the life of God. But we are also *Christs*—without the apostrophe. Pure exhortation! Just as Christ bears the burden of our sin and brokenness with us and for us, we are called to do the same for our neighbor. How do we enter into solidarity with those around us and help them carry their load? Furthermore, we bear witness to Christ when we understand that it is not we who stand with our neighbor, but Christ through us. Finally, we are Christs when we proclaim the forgiveness of God and the promise of abundant and eternal life, for in fact, Christ is speaking the Word through us in the very act!

Ultimately, viewing our baptism as a calling is vastly different from volunteering as a part of our faith life. Volunteering puts us at the center in a semi-heroic fashion. Being called as Christ's and as Christs is something entirely different, for God is clearly at the center of things.

Reflection and conversation: processing what you've learned

1. How did Terry's story make you feel? What difference does it make for you if you see life as an opportunity to make a positive difference for others?

---

2. Does it make sense to you why baptism is a new creation, a second creation?

_____

_____

_____

3. How do you regard your baptism? Is it mainly an event long ago for you with little significance for today, or is it an ongoing source of strength and encouragement for you? Why or why not?

_____

_____

_____

4. How do you experience the battle between the old and new self? Does it surprise you that the old self is a good swimmer? Does it discourage you?

_____

_____

_____

5. Have you ever thought about your baptism as a calling to nourish your growth and to experience God through your fellow Christian? What is your calling to be a part of the body of Christ?

_____

_____

_____

6. Have you ever thought about your baptism as a calling to nourish your fellow brother or sister in Christ's growth, to build up the body of Christ?

_____

_____

_____

7. What difference does it make for you that Jesus offers the joyful exchange to you?

_____

_____

_____

8. How does it make you feel that you, in turn, can offer the joyful exchange to your neighbor or family member? How might you bear witness to this good news?

_____

_____

_____

9. How might you show your neighbor that you are helping them bear their burden? How might you show them that someone bigger than you is bearing that burden, too?

_____

_____

_____

10. Have you ever had the experience of Christ ministering to you through a neighbor, even one who may have minimal Christian connection?

_____

_____

_____

11. When do you experience calling as duty, i.e., when you don't feel like it?

_____

_____

_____

Wrap-up

What questions do you have as we end this chapter?

_____

_____

_____

What takeaways do you have?

_____

_____

_____

I believe God provides all the gifts necessary
for the future that God prefers and promises
each local church.

—*Patrick Keifert, We Are Here Now*

Spiritual gifts, then, are evidence or a
demonstration that God's Holy Spirit is
working in us, enabling us to do things we
could not otherwise do.

—*David Stark, LifeKeys*

CHAPTER 9

THE GIFTS FOR BUILDING UP THE CHURCH

Review and reflection

Christian faith is not about improving on our mistakes. It's about dying and rising to a new reality, a new creation—Jesus Christ. However, there is an ongoing tension and paradox we must live with. The death and birth of baptism are simultaneous, at once announcing a new reality—but a reality that has not yet come to full fruition. Thus, we remain in the fallen world (and it remains in us) and we are dying to it, quite literally, but have already been released from its claim on us. Indeed, baptized believers—through the joyful exchange with Jesus Christ—have been grafted into a new world. And so, while our old self still struggles in the grips of this world, at the same time, we seek to nourish the new self, born into a new creation. Death and new life then become daily rhythms of life for the baptized.

From a vocational theology perspective, the dying and rising of baptism is both gift and calling. Just as we receive the benefits of this new creation—forgiveness, abundant life, and community—we simultaneously become channels through which this new life is shared with others. *We are Christ's, with and without the apostrophe*, for we have been reborn as members of the new creation in Christ. Interestingly, just as we were gifted in the first creation with our natural abilities, so, too, are we gifted once again in the new creation.

What resonates with you from chapter 8, where we examined baptism as both membership and calling in a new creation?

_____

_____

_____

What lingering questions do you have from chapter 8?

_____

_____

_____

CHAPTER OVERVIEW

Being members of the body of Christ—which is another name for the Christian Church—we continue the work of God in the world through Christ. Even as God's victory over sin, death, and the power of evil is assured in Christ—and one day God's work will fully come to fruition—the ongoing work of God in the world continues through the church. It is important to stress that when we refer to the church, we mean all baptized believers (the saints referred to in Ephesians). For us, then, there is work to do, and we are equipped for it. Christ—by the power of the Holy Spirit—gives each member of the body gifts to be used to "equip the saints for the work of ministry, for building up the body of Christ." (Eph 4:11-12). The New Testament word for these gifts is, once again, charism (plural charismata), which refers not only to those who today we would say have charisma, but to a wide range of gifts. These gifts would be mostly functional, and useful, but uncharismatic in the modern sense. While these gifts may build upon the natural abilities God gave us at birth, spiritual gifts transcend natural abilities; they are born of life experience and finetuned by the Holy Spirit for our role(s) within the church. These gifts are given for the special purpose of strengthening the church's work and witness in the world as part of the ongoing missio Dei—mission of God. Or, as Paul stressed in his epistles, spiritual gifts are to be used in love and for that purpose only—never to advance oneself or status. This chapter will focus on the nature of the church's work in the world, the roles we are called to within the church, and the gifts upon which our roles are based.

Introduction to the gifts for building up the church

Sometimes film and literature offer us metaphorical glimpses of key themes found in scripture. Such is the case with a monumental work of literature in the twentieth century that also became a blockbuster cinematic event just after the turn of the century. In this case, some of the dynamics of the formation of the Christian Church are dramatized vividly!

> **FILM CLIP**
>
> In the movie, *The Fellowship of the Ring*, a fellowship is formed around a mission to eradicate a great evil. The scene at the Council of Elrond is a metaphorical synopsis of the Christian Church. It is no accident, perhaps, since the writer of *The Lord of the Rings*, J. R. R. Tolkien, was a stanch Catholic. As the members of the fellowship feel called to step forward and engage in mission, one by one, they each recognize they have a gift to offer. So, as they step forward, they pledge their gift and unique skill to the fellowship and the cause. While it is not clear where they will go and what they will do next, they have faith that a wise wizard, Gandalf, will show them the way.[1] The themes of fellowship, gifts, calling, mission, and discernment are all in this scene. May we in the church learn from these fictional characters of Middle Earth!

LEARNING: FINDING YOUR PLACE IN THE BODY OF CHRIST

WHAT IS THE *CHURCH*?

The church is the body of Christ, reconstituted not as one human being—Jesus—but as a *fellowship*. No mere fellowship of nine (as in *The Lord of the Rings*), this fellowship numbers millions who have been grafted into a new creation. This new creation, of course, is first and foremost a body—the body of Jesus Christ, and now a community of witnesses.

---

1 Jackson, *Fellowship*, 1:26:45–1:33:42.

Bound together by the body and blood of Jesus and empowered by the Holy Spirit, this community is formed to continue the work of Jesus of Nazareth on earth and bear witness to a future that is in God's hands. As such, we continue God's commitment and ongoing mission to a broken creation. To this end, each of us is equipped by the Holy Spirit with gifts to utilize for the sake of building up the body of Christ so that it may robustly engage its call and mission. Indeed, by means of the Holy Spirit, Jesus remains God's incarnation in the world *through us*. Surely, none of us *is Jesus*, and yet through Jesus the community of God has been extended to us, breaking down the barrier between God and created matter, forming a new creation. We are Christs on account of our relationship with Christ, who is alive in and through us.

Sometimes people debate what constitutes "the church." Historically, the church has always been defined as a people gathered in faith around Word and sacrament—a people with a clearly defined center. That center is the living Word, Jesus Christ. Sacraments are the way that we tangibly take hold of God's gifts of being born into the body of Christ and being nourished by God's presence. However, the church that gathers around Word and sacrament is a community formed expressly for mission—in other words, to be *sent*. Indeed, by the power of the Holy Spirit, God's incarnate Word is a movement to redeem lost lives, restore health and wholeness, and create a more trustworthy world. To be a church member is to be a part of this movement, for the church is not an institution; it is an event. It is alive and purposefully in motion. And so, the church is not a *place* you go to, but a *movement* you join—God's movement. It therefore consists of people. So, you don't really *go* to church, you *are* the church. The church is the church *gathered* around God's Word and *sent* by God's Word into the world. It is fair, in sum, to say that the Christian Church is defined by its clear center—Jesus Christ—and its porous boundaries with the world around it. For it is that world to which the church is sent.

The church lives in two creations

The church is, first and foremost, an expression and sign of the new creation. The work of the church is to bear witness—to point—to the new creation while striving to embody that new creation; in other words, to show it, however imperfectly that may be. It is uniquely the work of the church to proclaim the Word incarnate, crucified, and risen. We are far beyond merely trying to be good people, bravely salvaging what we can from a lost world. We are leaning into a *new* one! And it could be argued that the new creation is nothing other than the fulfillment of the Ten Commandments—God's prescriptive Word about love's manifestation.

But the Commandments cannot create love, or righteous people. The new creation in Christ offers not only the promise of love's fulfillment in human history, but also a robust vision of what human existence looks like, that is based on God's unconditional promises. God's kingdom and will *will* be done, and this promise of abundant life is *for us*.

Nonetheless, the church affirms both creations as realms where God is at work. In church history since the Reformation, leaders and clergy have often misrepresented the two creations theology (what Luther called "two kingdoms") by separating them.[2] As this fallacious reasoning goes, if the second creation is the creation that fully expresses God's will, it is also something in the future, when God will bring God's kingdom to fruition. Meanwhile, we shouldn't expect too much from our current, highly compromised world. So, let the environment choke on carbon emissions, don't sweat the inequalities that plague our societies, and accept the ways of the world. This world's a lost cause, anyway. In the new creation in the distant future, God will make things right. So, we should just chill for now. It should be pointed out that such false reasoning is usually expressed by those who are benefiting from the status quo!

This is a misreading of the two creations. It is the heart and soul of the Christian message that God's new creation in Christ is nothing less than the meaning, purpose, and aim of human history, i.e., the first creation. Therefore, while the two creations are to be distinguished, they are not to be separated! The church is called to foster hope, then, by pointing to the fruition of God's second creation as the ultimate end point of human history, while also diligently practicing the values of God's kingdom, trusting that God's creation in Christ will transform the world we know. This means the church does not look the other way when our natural world is being destroyed and human rights violated. Far from it. We bear witness to another way.

And so, the church is a community formed by God for a mission: the proclamation that God has promised to deliver each of us from sin, death, and the power of evil. The full expression of this is in the future when the second creation is fully manifest. The church could be viewed as a down payment on that promise. (Do others around us see evidence of this down payment that has been made?) But the immediate result of this proclamation of God's promise of a sure and certain future can evoke faith in those who hear it. So we must learn how, as a church, to find the language—and sometimes the nerve—to share our faith in this promise.

---

2 Braaten, *Principles*, 123-38.

Doing so can instill much-needed faith in the listener now, so we are not only concerned with future outcomes, but also present ones.

While it is true that the church is anchored in the second creation, nonetheless, every congregation is also a human institution and very much an expression of the old creation as well. That means we function in many of the same ways as other human institutions—with the same limitations and dysfunctions. But God is used to working with flawed mediums, like each of us, for instance. And so it is that God can work through church bodies that don't always reflect what the body of Christ means.

It is also true that because God created the first creation and is still at work in it, the church is called to join God there, co-creating a more trustworthy world by listening to and loving our neighbors. This is part of the second calling of the baptized that we discussed in the last session. Loving our neighbor means not only loving them in the private dimensions of their lives, but in the public dimensions, too. It's been said that justice is what love looks like in the public arena. That means we are called to the work of peacemaking and justice, and as we do so, we are also bearing witness to the second creation. Notions such as ensuring there are food and essentials for everyone are all about loving your neighbor in the first creation, to be sure, but they also bear witness to the new creation, where everyone has enough. The same is true in working for peace and developing cultures of life, not death. As we do so, we bear witness to the new creation, where swords are beaten into plowshares. The truth is, the biblical material we have at our fingertips that describes God's kingdom (or creation) has often been at the forefront of history-making movements for peace and justice.

Gifts of the Spirit to "equip the saints"

Ephesians tells us that gifts are given to "equip the saints for building up the body of Christ" (Eph 4:12). The saints referred to are a bit more numerous than the Roman Catholic definition of sainthood allows since all the baptized are the saints! Each of the saints is equipped with a charism, or gift of the Spirit, to strengthen the church and its mission in the world. It is worth noting the close connection between this concept and Luther's doctrine of the priesthood of all believers. The power of the church is not to be found in clergy or paid staff, but in the members who do the work of God according to their many and various callings—and are equipped for such callings.

Once again, we are gifted for the creation of which we are a part. In the first creation, as we learned, each of us is equipped with natural abilities that give us a clue as to what God might be up to in our lives. In the new creation in Christ, likewise, we are equipped for a new creation. In this one, the creation is God's own body into which we have been grafted as members, thanks to the joyful exchange. While God first created *through* Christ (John 1:3), in the second creation, God created *in* Christ, for in the person of Jesus of Nazareth, God's kingdom has been made manifest. Christ is the first fruit of all who will be made alive *in* Christ (I Corinthians 15:23). One person, sure, but many persons make up this body, which is a vast community, and we are equipped precisely for the building up of this body, as Paul writes in Ephesians.

"Building up" here refers to nurturing and empowering the church for the missio Dei, which means to reconcile the fallen world with God so that all may be released from the bondage of sin and decay and experience the fullness of life. In short, the church exists so that the world might be transformed in the new creation through a restored relationship of trust—or faith—in God. For this reason, we are gifted by Christ and through the power of the Spirit with charisms, so that we will discern our roles within the body of Christ for the sake of missio Dei. Within this body, this church, all members have special callings based on the spiritual gifts they have been given.

The spiritual gifts in the New Testament are the tip of the iceberg

The gifts that are identified in the New Testament include the following from I Corinthians 12: wisdom, knowledge, faith, healing, miracles, prophecy, discernment, tongues, interpretation of tongues, apostles, prophets, teachers, deeds of power, assistance, and leadership. It should be noted that apostles, prophets, and teachers are terms that designate roles or callings more than gifts, but the implication is clearly that gifts are given to equip members for the roles they play, so there is an interchangeable nature here. If we are equipped for a role, we have been given the gifts necessary for it. What is noteworthy in the church at Corinth is that the context of healing divisions within the church calls for gifts of a more inward focus. That will not be the case in Ephesians.

In Ephesians 4:1-16, we learn that the gifts Christ gave were that some would be apostles, prophets, evangelists, pastors, and teachers, for the purpose of equipping the saints—seemingly an allusion to a whole host of other gifts that those in leadership positions will help elicit. The addition of *evangelist* indicates a more outward focus of mission than was the case in Corinth. And in Romans 12:3-8, the gifts of prophecy, ministry, teaching, exhortation, generosity, leadership, and compassion are repeated from the other lists, with the addition of ministry, exhortation, generosity and compassion.

Now, it must be said that the gift of speaking in tongues, and perhaps the gift of interpreting tongues seems like a strange gift to some of us in the Lutheran church. Of course, the original purpose of speaking in tongues (and still for some) was to celebrate the ecstatic experience of the Holy Spirit at work within someone. When you think about it, that is what the church is all about, namely, a people filled with the presence (Holy Spirit) of God! After all, a crucial aspect of the new creation is that the Holy Spirit is active in leading and shaping the lives of church members. So we ought not be critical of speaking in tongues in a knee-jerk manner. Likewise, gifts like miracles and healing also seem a bit *out there* to many, yet they too are a testament to the belief that the living God is at work among us as a healing force who is capable of extraordinary things that defy explanation. Perhaps we are all called to be open to this extraordinary dimension that comes with being a Christian.

Rounding out the gifts that are of a very spiritual nature, prophecy, discernment, and faith are all explicitly focused on our relationship with the transcendent and immanent God. And while faith and discernment are gifts that are given in some measure to all people in Christian fellowship, for some, these gifts are more exceptional. These gifts serve as a reminder that the church is not merely a human institution of do-gooders. It is indeed rooted in something transcendent and unfathomable that has nonetheless touched down among us and in us.

On the other hand, we all recognize the gifts that are not exclusively spiritual—but equally vital—which include teaching, apostleship (those who are sent), assisting, and compassion. These gifts are interesting in that a person of faith is called to *all of these* in some measure within the specific contexts of a person's life. Everyone has some wisdom to pass on and teach in a spirit of love. Everyone is sent into the world, called to exercise compassion, and assist with those around them. To some extent, then, the charismata are reminders of what we are all called to be about. Nonetheless, the gifts of the Spirit are given in special measure to each of us to help us identify our roles and callings in our Christian faith community. Revisiting our status as creatures with finite lives, such gifts as these, given within the new creation, help us focus and not attempt to be all things all once. In other words, the gifts of the Spirit are deeply contextual and emerge out of our unique personhood and story.

There are twenty or so gifts that are identified in the pages of the New Testament, but the exact number is not important or relevant. Here's why: as noted by New Testament scholar J. Paul Sampley, lists of the gifts we find in Ephesians, I Corinthians, and Romans are not meant to be *exhaustive* but *illustrative*.[3] The lists, and their differences, illustrate that rather than the charismata being a set list, they are specially crafted capacities cultivated by the Holy Spirit *from* each person's crucible of life and *for* a particular context with specific challenges. That means there is no limit to the number of charismata that are possible. One has a clear impression of God creating ever-evolving variations of giftedness that build upon a person's natural gifts, life experiences, ethnicity, socioeconomic status, and the situation in which they are called. We are a people called to bear witness to and embody God's new creation and its values. Whatever is most helpful for each person serves as the basis for how the Word of God is applied to real life situations. The Holy Spirit is at work, always, to bring about the building up of life in ways relevant to how people live and love, hope, and suffer.

The necessary guiding value for all charismata: love

There is another crucial aspect to be observed about spiritual gifts: they are always to be employed in love. Paul's famous reflection on spiritual gifts in I Corinthians 12 is anchored immediately in chapter 13 with a sweeping meditation on love. And they are linked for a most important reason. The Church at Corinth had fallen into misunderstanding and misuse of the charismata, gifts of the Spirit. For many of the Corinthians, such gifts had become the basis for division and social hierarchy, wherein some gifts were regarded more highly than others, often aligning with and reinforcing socioeconomic differences within the church as well. Those who had the more coveted and high-ranking gifts were inclined to lose their humility, regarding their spiritual gift as validation of a higher spirituality or importance. In particular, the gift of tongues was thought to be the pinnacle of gifts possessed by those who could utter the strange, ecstatic sounds of the Holy Spirit. Understandably, this fostered feelings of false pride, resentment, and ultimately, a misplaced focus on the wrong things. The charismata are not given to puff up some individuals (but not

---

3 Sampley, Interpreter's Bible Commentary, 817.

others) with a sense of pride and superiority. As Paul points out forcefully in these verses, spiritual gifts are given not for self-aggrandizement, but for the sake of love and always to be employed in love. "If I speak in the tongues of mortals and of angels, but do not have love, I am a noisy gong or a clanging cymbal" (I Cor 13:1).

It is a worthy reminder at this point that Paul's description of love here is a beautiful description of *agape* love in that it is distinguished not by intensity of feeling or emotion, but by a person's commitment in spirit and will to do that which upbuilds others' lives. When one reads the description of love in I Corinthians 13:4-7, it is striking how unemotional love seems. It's not about conjuring an emotion that moves one to action, but rather about such qualities as patience, kindness, and not insisting on one's own way. All charismata are guided and in service to the meta-value called love which consistently seeks the well-being of the other, regardless of one's feelings toward that person.

Paul also took great pains in his letter to the Ephesians to stress that every gift is valuable—there was no hierarchy of gifts. To illustrate this, he compared the gifts and roles of each person in the church to the parts of the body, where no part is unnecessary. Rather, all parts are there for a reason, and that reason must be honored. This reinforces the original meaning of charisma, which affirms that the gifts of the Spirit do indeed come in many forms, and include the gifts that do not align with the current use of the word charisma. Just as our discussion of personality revealed, the less showy and magnetic persons and their gifts are equally valuable in the scheme of things, and without a doubt, in the world of the church. I suppose if charisma in the modern sense refers to one's capacity to move, captivate, or influence another person, we would have to say that all of the charismata can be utilized to do that in their own, albeit more subtle, ways. Namely, make a difference in someone else's life for the better!

It is rightfully argued that Paul's use of the aim of our gifts and callings to build up the body of Christ is nothing other than another way of talking about love. What is useful to strengthen the fellowship of believers and its work in the world? What helps the community to be healthy, strong, and in alignment with that for which it is created? Love. Love always works to upbuild the life—individual or corporate—of that which has been made through Christ (John 1) or in Christ (I Cor 15). Paul was attempting to help the Corinthians refocus on love and a higher calling, just as he was steering them away from self and their own struggles with incurvatus. This, too, is our guiding value of values—as we discussed in chapter 4—in all our callings. Our gifts, no matter what they may be, are to be used in love, or not at all.

In this singular and unique body of people called the church, where do you fit in? What gifts has the Spirit bequeathed to you? What are your callings in your congregation?

SUMMARY

The Christian Church is the body of Christ, a community of baptized believers formed by God to carry on the work of Jesus and the missio Dei in the world, which necessarily includes bearing witness to the new creation in Christ. It is defined by both *gathering* and *sending*, namely, gathering members around the presence of God and sending them to *be* the church in the world with whomever they are gathered. The Christian Church is called to a clear center—Christ—with porous boundaries around its fellowship, thereby increasing interaction between the church and the world. The church exists in two creations, old and new, affirming both as realms where God is at work. While continuing the work of creating a trustworthy world and loving one's neighbor, the church is also called to both embody and bear witness to the new creation in Christ.

This work of the church and its members is aided by the charismata, the gifts given by Christ through the Holy Spirit to each member of Christ's Church. It is not unlike the gifts employed by each member in forging a new fellowship to preserve a life-giving world in *The Lord of the Rings* trilogy. So, as natural gifts are given to each of us in the first creation of Genesis, gifts are also given to each in the new creation to strengthen the church's work and witness. Mostly described in the writings of Paul, these gifts are potentially innumerable, as they are forged and refined by the Spirit from one's natural abilities, combined with life experience and current context. One's gifts must never be an occasion for boasting or advancing self-interest, but are rather to be used in the interests of building up the body of Christ, which is to say, for love.

Reflection and conversation

1. Is the definition of church as *relationship* and *event* instead of an institution and place new to you? What difference does it make?

_____

_____

_____

2. What are the challenges or obstacles to bearing witness to the second creation (the kingdom of God)—to the God who delivers us from sin, death, and the power of evil? How might we think about doing this in natural, organic, loving ways that are not pretentious or self-righteous?

_____

_____

_____

3. Why do you think the church sometimes struggles with addressing and acting on peace and justice issues (what love looks like in the public sector)?

_____

_____

_____

4. What do you think of having gifts of the Spirit in addition to natural abilities? Can you see the difference?

_____

_____

_____

5. If you were to try and discern what your spiritual gift(s) might be as you look at your role in your faith community, what gifts do you identify? Think of one or two listed in Ephesians or I Corinthians and then one or two that is something more original to you and your lived experience.

_____

_____

_____

6. How do you think your spiritual gifts match up with your history of participation at your church? Have you utilized your gifts extensively? What is one time when you feel your gifts were used very well and it was satisfying to you?

_____

_____

_____

7. To which of your spiritual gifts do you feel the most drawn? Why?

_____

_____

_____

8. Allowing yourself to brainstorm for a few moments, what new ideas come to mind regarding how God might be calling you in the future to serve in your faith community?

_____

_____

_____

9. How can you discern what God wants you to do at church *now*? How can you establish boundaries around this, so that you don't overcommit at church, also knowing that the most time—and labor—intensive callings are outside of church?

_____

_____

_____

Wrap up

What questions do you have about Chapter 9?

_____

_____

_____

What takeaways do you have from Chapter 9?

_____

_____

_____

What are you going to do, now that you don't
have to do anything?

—*Gerhard Forde, Justification by Faith*

CHAPTER 10

THE GIFT OF THE FREEDOM TO BE YOU

Review and reflection

In the formation of the Christian Church, we see missio Dei quite dramatically laid out before our eyes. God's mission to a lost world is nothing other than the triune God in bold action. Working as the interactive community that God is, we see that community stretching itself in love toward the world. God the Father creates the world out of love, only to watch the spirit of loving community with which it was created discarded in favor of individualism and self-justification. The Father then sends the incarnate Son to redeem the world by extending God's fellowship to human beings, and through his death and resurrection, birthing a new creation. The Father and the Son then together send the Holy Spirit to unleash the transforming power of God in the world and into the hearts of baptized believers (and into the world upon all flesh!). Last, the Father, Son and Holy Spirit form and send the church into the world to bear witness to the coming kingdom of God and engage in the fullness of the missio Dei. Bearing witness to this truth in speech and action is our mission, and for this mission and new creation, we have been equipped all over again.

In this new creation, adherents must remember the central truth of their new existence, namely, that their mission is made possible by the very truth that frees us to love our neighbor: we are justified by God's grace alone, and not by any efforts of our own.

What resonated with you from Chapter 9 and our discussion of the nature of the church and spiritual gifts?

_____

_____

_____

What would you like to explore some more?

_____

_____

_____

CHAPTER OVERVIEW

The single greatest teaching of Luther and the foundation of the Reformation is this simple phrase: "Justification by grace through faith." As a result, we are reconciled with God, and reborn through baptism as a part of God's new creation in Christ. So, not only do we have a different relationship with God, but we also have a different relationship with our world and with life itself, for we no longer need this life and this world to justify ourselves. My justification, then, is both a gift to me and my neighbor. Without the freedom we receive from God's unconditional embrace, we remain prisoners to our quest for self-justification and all the forms it takes in this life. Not only is self-justification futile for the broken sinner, but it prevents each of us from truly loving our neighbor. In baptism, this broken life is no longer the source of meaning, wholeness, and belonging, for these things are unconditionally given to us by a loving God and promised to us in the new creation. The promises of God justify us and disarm all forms of brokenness. We are then free to do what we were meant to do: love our neighbor and embrace the community of creation. In this session, we will examine the ways that our callings are directly connected to our freedom in Christ.

Introduction to the gift of freedom

I've observed over the years that people in the congregations and youth groups I've served have an objection to deathbed conversions. You know, if someone accepts Jesus and comes to faith on their deathbed. The criticism of this kind of divine justice goes as follows: So-and-so didn't even have to live like a Christian and try to obey the Commandments, but they still got into heaven. It's not fair!

The idea behind this sentiment is obvious. Salvation shouldn't be completely free. On some level, Christians should have to pay their dues.

But there's another idea lurking here that is also important. Having faith without showing it in love and actions doesn't seem right, either. Someone on their deathbed doesn't have a chance to show their faith (much), but people who live their lives claiming to be Christians do have that chance. If they fail to demonstrate compassion, humility, and integrity, it becomes problematic. As Christians, we're supposed to be good, loving people.

Lutherans believe that salvation is entirely a gift, no strings attached. There are no good works that you can do or need to do to be saved from sin, death, and the power of evil. And the first objection to this is often, Well, why should I do anything good, then? Why not do whatever you feel like, because you're going to heaven anyway!

There are legitimate questions about a faith tradition that teaches salvation as a gift, and one of them is the relationship between faith and acts of service and love. Ultimately, faith must lead to love and good works in a person's life. Most people can affirm the importance of this outcome of faith. Luther was accused in his theology of taking away the motivation, the lever, for doing good works. That lever, of course, was the threat of eternal damnation unless you were a good enough Christian.

His response? Not only are good works important, but he was going to show his critics how good works are *possible*! For Luther, good works were not remotely possible until they became untethered from the motivation to do good works to advance one's standing with God. The answer for Luther lay in the fact that true acts of love for your neighbor are done not to accumulate points for yourself, because then your actions are done not for your neighbor's benefit, but for your own. True acts of love are those actions done for the benefit of my neighbor, not me. So, if our faith makes us truly free from ourselves and our need to justify ourselves, we are also free to love our neighbor because our neighbor needs it. That is why it's critical to stress that good works in a person's life are a *result* of salvation, not a *prerequisite* or condition.

So then, why love your neighbor when grace already has you covered? There is only one answer that matters here: you love your neighbor because your neighbor needs love!

LEARNING: CALLINGS BASED ON JUSTIFICATION BY GRACE THROUGH FAITH

Good works in Luther's time: why love needs freedom

In Luther's time, it was believed that faith was perfected in love. While faith was a sign of God's grace, love was the follow-through, and that was on the shoulders of the one who professed faith. The bottom line was that faith alone was not enough to save a person. Faith needed love, i.e., good works, for the believer to become acceptable to God.

One can see this theology at work in the biblical metaphor of marriage in the New Testament, wherein Christ is the groom who marries and saves the broken sinner (you and me), who is the bride. This marriage forms the church, a sign and expression of the new creation in Christ. But Catholic theology in Luther's time held that the bride of Christ must be made pure before the wedding can occur. So, the bride had to become righteous to be acceptable. This was then a lifelong journey to attain such righteousness. God gives you some grace and some faith, but then it is your turn: use it or it will be taken away. Produce good works and love your neighbor so that you can rack up enough points—enough righteousness—to rise to the level of acceptability to God. There is grace here because you can't do it without God's help, but you better do your part, or you'll be stuck in purgatory—or worse!

For Luther, the metaphor of marriage was one way of speaking of the previously discussed joyful exchange that takes place between Christ and the sinner. But he looked at this marriage far differently than his Catholic brethren. For Luther, in a marriage, all assets and liabilities are shared—not unlike today. In the marriage of God and broken people, Christ then takes on their shame, rebellion, guilt, despair, and doubt as his own. In return, he bestows upon her what she lacks: healing, forgiveness, abundant life, community, and a clean conscience. In other words, through Christ the bride becomes righteous. It is not *her own* righteousness, though. It has been given to her, conferred to her from outside herself. Hence, Luther referred to this as *alien* righteousness.

The Catholics objected to this idea, saying that Luther was suggesting that Christ would actually marry a bride who *clearly had issues!* She (which would be you and I) was not worthy of marrying Christ.[1] But this was Luther's point: no, she wasn't worthy, and neither are we—ever. But Jesus is worthy, and that's enough. God has chosen to count us as righteous by association with the bridegroom. He is, after all, the savior, so that is where our trust and focus is. And when our trust is in the righteousness of Christ, and not our own, that same righteousness will show up in your life—in gratitude, in generosity, in love!

Why unconditional promise is so important

Christian tradition has always held that not only are we as human beings collectively a bride with issues, but we are dependent on what Christ brings to the marriage. In the matter of our salvation, there is nothing whatsoever we bring to make it happen. Even cooperating with God in salvation was considered a heresy. It is God's work alone that saves us. And this is possible because of a unique kind of authority God has: The authority to make an unconditional promise.

There are two kinds of authority that God—or anyone—has: *if-then* authority, and *because-therefore* authority.[2] The difference between these two is important. If-then authority is conditional authority and establishes parameters whereby I seek to direct you by narrowing your options. Parents use this with their kids frequently: *If* you don't eat your carrots, *then* you will not get to watch TV. Or, if-then authority can be a descriptive authority, stating the way things are: If you overeat, then you will gain weight. God's law and the world work with this kind of authority, one of conditions and consequences. So, if you steal from your neighbor, then there will be consequences—both for him and you. Among the consequences could be guilt, distrust, anger, retaliation, and arrest. In a word, pain, in any number of ways. With if-then authority, there are always conditions that modify and limit one's future. If-then authority is not bad, it's good, but it can't save you when the consequences and conditions become unmanageable.

---

1 Kolb, Genius, 47.
2 Gritsch and Jensen, *Lutheranism*, 8.

Then there is the authority of unconditional promise, wherein one's promise is a commitment that opens up a future possibility for you. So, for instance, I might say to you, Because I love you, I will pay for your schooling.

Most people think our relationship with God is based on if-then authority; God says to us, If you obey my commandments, then I will save you. Consequently, we may hope that we've done our part and will be judged favorably in the end. Unfortunately though, even if we believe our salvation is a free gift, we often put a condition on it: If you accept Jesus into your heart, then you will be saved. That's all you have to do, the only condition. However, it must be pointed out that when we adopt this construction we have rejected the unconditional character of God's promise. Salvation now depends on you, not God.

Luther taught that God's promises are unconditional, which means they are of the because-therefore kind of authority. This is the gospel message and it is good news, indeed! For we human beings who are not Jesus, the conditions on the ground always rob us of true life and a future. These conditions include our lack of faith, our sin, and death. However, if the one making the promise takes on these conditions as his own, this opens up an unconditional future for the other. By taking these conditions upon God's own self through Jesus, all the conditions that destroy our future are removed: sin and death.

And the only one with the authority or power to make a truly unconditional promise is God, who alone can remove all conditions that bind the future.

No matter how much we may want to try, human beings cannot make an unconditional promise because there are too many things that we cannot control. Even wedding vows are modified by what condition? *Until death parts us.* The parent who promises to pay for schooling also cannot do so unconditionally. That parent might go bankrupt or die. Only God can remove all the conditions that limit your future. Because God loves us and sent his only Son to die, therefore, we have been set free from sin and death. A person can trust this proclamation or walk away.

Sometimes God's forgiveness is extended in a human context when someone bears the conditions as their own so that another can be set free. Such was the case in a fictional retelling of a bounty hunter of slaves in the eighteenth-century, who then faced the tribe he plundered. This may be fiction, but it reveals a painful amount of human history in the process.

FILM CLIP

In the movie, *The Mission*, there is a scene of astounding power and beauty. During the colonial years in South America, Spain and Portugal were trafficking in slavery there. A man named Rodrigo (played by Robert DeNiro) is a particularly notorious mercenary who captures and sells slaves. At one point, Rodrigo's life of rage and brutality breaks him and he repents of his slave-trading sins. Yet, the forgiveness he really seeks is from the tribe of native peoples he has terrorized. Advised by the local missionary and priest who works with the native peoples, Rodrigo engages in his version of penance, carrying around the weight of the tools of his trade in a bag. The bag is heavy—just like his guilt—made up of sword, shield, armor, and so on. He risks his life dragging this load up the slippery rocks of a giant waterfall, up and down muddy hills until finally he is face-to-face with those from whom he has stolen human capital. There, the leader of the tribe approaches him with a knife, and we know full well that if Rodrigo gets what he deserves, his throat will be slit.

And yet an execution is not what happens. Instead, after verbally accosting Rodrigo, the leader cuts the rope, freeing his heavy bag of weapons and armor, then pushes it down the cliff into the river. Washed away! Rodrigo's sins are forgiven. The weight of his sins and the conditions of his horrific past have been borne by those he hurt most. It dawns on him that he is now free from his guilt. He has been born again. Now he can remain and love these people, which is exactly what he does. His existence and life have heretofore been justified and given back to him to start over.[3]

THE LIGHTBULB OF FREEDOM

I was teaching a class once where the topic was the unconditional gift of God's promises. We were discussing how this world is defined by conditions—as we've discussed—while God's gift of salvation is freely given. Jesus died and rose, freeing you from the power of sin and death. Period. There are no conditions to be met. God has already met all the conditions for you!

The question arose, "Well, don't you have to believe it, accept it in faith?"

---

3 Joffé, *The Mission*, 39:09—42:35.

To which I responded, "It is true that faith must be present for the promise to be redeemed, for salvation to occur."

"Well, isn't that a condition? You have to accept the offer!"

My response? "The minute you make it a condition that has to be met, it is no longer unconditional. Suddenly, there is something you have to do, and you are right to wonder over and over again if you have successfully met that condition. 'Do I believe enough? Do I have the right kind of faith? What about the days I am filled with doubts?' The good news is that you don't need to worry. It's all been taken care of by Jesus. It's pure gift. Believe it, trust it."

And the truth is, if we do believe it and trust it, this is itself a gift because we are not capable of conjuring faith on our own. It can only be created when God's promise for me is proclaimed to me and stirs up faith within me. It is created, then, from the action of God's Word for me and in me. This also demonstrates the fallacy of decision theology, which insists that to be saved, we must make a decision. But think about this for a moment. This is, arguably, the most important decision in life. If someone decides to give their life to Christ, then faith *was already present* in that person. One would never entrust their life to a particular deity unless they already knew in their heart that this God was trustworthy! And how did their heart arrive at that state of trust? More of a wonder and mystery, perhaps? It is a gift! Not a decision.

The belief, trust, or faith we experience is not a condition to be met, but a description of a new relationship, a relationship of trust. Faith, then, is a *state of being* describing the new relationship. When faith is positioned as a condition to be met, it puts all the focus on me and leaves the whole transaction pending on whether I generated enough faith. And of course, it also leaves me in control of sealing the deal on my salvation, and that need for control is exactly the problem.

At that point in the class, Ken stood up and said, "I think I get it! If there is nothing I have to do, but it's all a gift, then I don't have to worry about myself and my fate. God has got my back. I'm completely free to go love my neighbor!"

And I said, "Yes, that's it, Ken! Here's your $20."

I promise he wasn't a plant. Ken just experienced the gift of an unanticipated revelation.

Because God loves you and sent his Son to this world, *therefore* you have been freed from the power of sin and death and given eternal life. And this has *everything* to do with our callings. Indeed, it makes callings possible because, in our new freedom, we are free for the neighbor. But the freedom we each experience will be experienced in different ways, and that is one of the keys to how we love our neighbor.

Pluripotent love, part I: *for me*

The Lutheran witness sinks or swims on one basic principle: justification by grace through faith. We've discussed how faith is the gift of a new relationship of trust established with God. And we've discussed how God exercises an unconditional, because-therefore, authority to create an unending future for us. This is grace, and it comes from God.

But what does it mean to be *justified*? Luther assumed that the greatest human need was to be justified with God, which meant to be in a right relationship—reconciled—with God. This normally entailed that the justified one must be declared righteous and upright. It could also be said that to be justified is to be made whole, authentic, and true to who we really are as human beings. It is a core Christian teaching that no one can justify oneself with God—even with the best intentions. We are too far down the rabbit hole of rebellion for that! Only God, and God alone, can save us. Hence, we live on as broken human beings, walking distortions of what we were intended to be. Knowing deep down that we are broken and guilty, the need for justification gnaws away at everyone, even those who do not identify the source of their plight.

Luther's insight was that justification took the form of unconditional forgiveness from God and set us free from worrying about our own status before God. For his Roman Catholic contemporaries, though, as we've discussed, justification meant a sort of provisional forgiveness. And if you were going to get more forgiveness down the road, you needed to accumulate merits and prove your worthiness, as we've seen. Again, your justification was then very much in *your* hands, not only in God's. And, I might add, it was very much in doubt. This contrast with what Luther taught will be critical when we turn to the matter of callings. One might think this whole discussion about justification has nothing to do with our callings, but that person would be wrong!

Before we consider our neighbor's needs, we must unpack the power of justification by grace through faith. In doing so, we understand far better how it is that God loves us and loves our neighbor through us. To be justified by grace through faith means not only being set free from bondage into life, it also means being released from burdens that greatly hinder our ability to love our neighbor. This release creates the freedom necessary to both consider—and respond to—our neighbor's needs with love. But if we do not consider ourselves justified, like most of Luther's contemporaries, then all our actions will be based on obtaining that elusive justification by accumulating points. Love then lapses into self-absorption. Without God's justifying Word in our lives, our brokenness presents a formidable barrier to loving our neighbor. This is why Luther took the opposite point of view of the prevailing axiom that "faith is perfected in love." Instead, suggested Luther, love is perfected in faith, for without a faith that frees us for love, love is a hollow, self-justifying exercise.

The whole idea of justification and callings becomes even more interesting when we consider that the need for justification can take many forms besides guilt and forgiveness. That means the unconditional promise each of us needs to hear might be articulated uniquely—and differently from the next person—because each of us experiences brokenness differently. And so, God's Word that is spoken out of love, that promises a life that is whole and eternal, will take different forms.

To borrow a medical term, God's love is analogous to "pluripotent" stem cells.[4] Pluripotent stem cells are special because they are potent in a plurality of ways. These cells, harvested in stem cell research and then transplanted to a new host, can become whatever they need to be, adapting to the needs of the living body into which they are placed. Hence, a pluripotent cell can become heart, liver, or brain tissue, as needed.

So, let's translate. Like a pluripotent stem cell, God's saving Word also takes whatever form is necessary to restore the broken life that hears it. For instance, in Luther's day, people experienced their broken relationship with God overwhelmingly through the feeling that they were guilty sinners. For a guilty sinner to be justified, then, meant to be forgiven by God of one's sin and guilt. That was what it meant to be set free. The quest for one's justification and atonement for one's sins had come to an end: Jesus took care of it! Now, one could put their own futile and angst-ridden efforts at self-justification behind them—and turn to their neighbor in love.

Yet many people today don't struggle with feeling like guilty sinners (which of course doesn't mean they aren't sinners), so their brokenness surfaces

---

4 Simpson, "'Putting on the Neighbor," 31-38.

in other ways. Rather than struggling with actions they've done that are wrong (guilt), people may be more prone to feeling shame, namely, the feeling that *they are wrong as a person* and that they are not worth much.[5] This feeling is reinforced by a culture that constantly judges the worth of people with all kinds of measuring sticks, from financial clout to social standing, to physical attractiveness, to athletic ability. Whether one is religious or not, the person who struggles with shame will inevitably live out their life desperately seeking ways to establish their value, make a name for themselves, or medicate their pain. So, for this person, who is battling shame in this way—and let's say is also a Christian—what becomes of the neighbor in their universe? The neighbor all too easily becomes an instrument, an object, to help them achieve a sense of worth. It's pretty hard to love our neighbor when we're consumed with shame and its effects, namely, desperately trying to *be someone* and alleviate the shame!

To the one who feels shame and worthlessness, God justifies her by declaring to her that she is of great worth to God. Her value is inestimable. This is grace, and this is an unconditional promise. Never again need she doubt her worth, her value as a human being. Of course, she will though, even if she comes to faith and her life is transformed. We all struggle with this sort of thing, but the point here is that justification by grace through faith means being valued by God, declared a pearl of inestimable worth, and believing it!

Do you think having faith that God deeply values you as a person might make a difference in how you see other people and interact with them? You don't need them to establish your worth. Rather, you can *love them.* Simply love them. If God values *you,* then surely God values *them,* too. God wants to free you from your self-preoccupation so that you can love your neighbor.

What other forms might justification take in our world? How do people experience their brokenness and alienation from God? For many, meaninglessness haunts them. One can only imagine how hard it is to love your neighbor if you think life has no meaning, that our actions on this earth have no meaning. That suffering goes unredeemed. That God has abandoned earthly affairs or never was there in the first place. Perhaps for this person, justification—reconciling his relationship with God—means being invited to participate in a world where everything matters, even the little things. It matters because God made this world and everything in it. It matters because God is invested in this world, actively involved in

---

5 Brown, *Culture of Shame*, xviii.

all things to redeem suffering and create a more life-giving, trustworthy, and hopeful world. It matters because God promises that life has the final word over death, hope over despair, and love over sin. And this same God offers the promise that you and I can be partners with God, working to bring forth life and bearing witness to the kingdom of God that will one day become fully manifest.

Do you think someone who comes to believe this promise will view their neighbor just a bit differently?

The last example I would like to note is the growing plight of loneliness, the state of not belonging. The person who experiences this emptiness will be searching their whole life for authentic connection, for a community of some sort. To the extent meaningful connections are not made, interactions with others will be driven, most likely, by the need to be accepted, not necessarily by the life-giving quality of the relationships. It is precisely this emotional profile that is most vulnerable to gang membership and hate-group participation. Gangs and hate groups *do* offer a sense of belonging and loyalty. What they *do not* offer is love. Jesus does offer love. Jesus tells us we've been made members of a family that will last forever.

Do you think that someone who hears and believes the good news that they belong to a family they can count on, a family that will last forever, will see their neighbor differently? They might have empathy for those who felt as they once did, desperately looking for acceptance and authentic relationships. And the justified person, the one whose relationship with God has been reconciled into a new community, that very same person might reach out in love.

The point of this section is simple: unless we are justified in our lives—in whatever form is relevant to us—we are hindered greatly in our ability to love. Why? Because we are primarily interested in seeking our justification and healing our wounds! So, then, hear the good news that you are justified in the ways you need to hear it, and give thanks. Then, with a grateful heart, you may actually love your neighbor.

What does a person need to become whole? Is it affirmation of their worth? Finding meaning in their existence and work? Discovering a community and relationships they can depend on? It's different for everyone. This brings to mind a familiar story that is known to us all, where each character needed something quite different ...

FILM CLIP

In the movie, *The Wizard of Oz*, our intrepid foursome reaches Oz and, ultimately, the wizard. For each of them, their quest is to become whole. The scarecrow lacks a brain, the tin man a heart, the lion courage, and Dorothy her home. When they finally learn the wizard is a fraud, he redeems himself somewhat by sagely understanding what each of them needs to feel complete; how their brokenness or emptiness took different forms in each of them. So, too, with us. Our broken relationship with God will manifest itself in different ways in each of us, and the good news of God's love for us is that it will provide precisely what each of us needs to be whole and to be free from the burden of our brokenness that will otherwise surely crush us.[6]

Pluripotent love, part II: for my neighbor

We've reflected at length on the pluripotent love of God that responds with good news that is appropriate to the many forms of brokenness that haunt us. Our justification then, by grace through faith, is a promise that we are free from the stifling inward curvature of life (incurvatus) and its many effects in the world that erode life. It also frees us to love our neighbor. We will now take up, however briefly, how we can channel that same message of pluripotent love for our neighbor—whatever that means to them. But we must make no mistake about where the healing love is coming from!

It's quite clear that if we are the bride who receives all of Christ's benefits (while Christ receives all our brokenness), we're the ones who married up, to say the least. It's also clear that with God's unconditional promise, all the work has been done for us. So, the natural reaction for us is to turn to God in adoration, awe, and trust, knowing that God is where righteousness comes from. Something happens when we turn to God in such a manner. A door opens, through which love flows freely from God through us into our lives and out toward others! All we can do is channel the good stuff that comes our way in faith. And so it is, that faith is active in love, and this love is not what we generate out of our good intentions. Rather, it is something that comes from God, and we participate in it. And as the very love of God flows through us to our neighbor, faith and love come together in a wonderful way. Luther said, "A Christian lives in Christ through faith, in his neighbor through love."[7] And because this

---

6 Fleming, *Wizard*, 1:29:13–1:32:41.
7 Luther quoted in Simpson, "Missional Congregations," 136.

love is not an action calculated by its benefit to me, it comes forth quite spontaneously from God as a gift to the neighbor.

What form does God's love in us take on for the sake of our neighbor? Galatians 5: 22–23 speaks of God's righteousness that produces the "fruit of the Spirit" in the believer. This fruit is of the Spirit because it is God's Holy Spirit that is the primary agency here. This metaphor is similar to the vine and branches imagery in John 15. The life of God in which we participate comes to us from beyond and becomes manifest, or embodied, in us as fruits of the Spirit. In Galatians 5, these fruits include love, joy, peace, patience, kindness, goodness, faithfulness, and self-control. Sometimes these fruits are referred to as *virtues*, as in the seven virtues of Roman Catholic tradition.

The truth is, there is only one fruit or virtue, namely love, for *God is love*. We were created by love for love. All other fruits and virtues are merely expressions of love that are appropriate to the context, hence, the many and varied potential fruit.[8] So, it is with God's love; it is pluripotent. Just as pluripotent love addresses our own form of brokenness, so too does it become the fruit, or virtue, that love of neighbor requires, namely, whatever is needed for their well being. With someone battling a terminal illness, love is patient. For someone who has been abused, love is kind. For someone who is rigid or depressed, love is joyful.

As we engage in our callings, we must always listen to what ails our neighbors so that we can understand what form love must take. Listen and discern what the *bad* news is before proclaiming the *good* news to them, for their justification may take a slightly different shape from your own. And remember, let the love that is flowing through you from God in Christ take the appropriate form in you for the sake of your neighbor in need. The fruits of the Spirit are always in the service of love. Significantly, Luther himself taught that a loving action for another can never be predetermined but must be discerned only after listening and assessing what my neighbor is going through.

---

8 Simpson, "'Putting on the Neighbor," 31-38.

SUMMARY

Justification by grace through faith is the foundational idea of the Reformation and the lynchpin of Luther's theology. This is often a hard truth to accept, as we are inclined to be suspicious of gifts freely given and would rather prove our worthiness somehow, which inevitably leads us down a road of self-absorption and incurvatus se. Only justification as a gift from outside ourselves can free us from this dead end and lead us into a life of abundance and love. It is often overlooked that justification not only frees a sinner for true life but also, by freeing them from their schemes of self-justification, frees the sinner for love of neighbor. For this reason, Luther made the case for the inversion of a classic Roman Catholic teaching. Rather than *faith perfected in love, love is perfected in faith*. Indeed, this is the only way love becomes possible.

The key to this kind of faith is made possible by God's unconditional promise of forgiveness and justification, meaning there are no conditions we as broken sinners must meet for the declaration to be true. God has met all the conditions, and in fact, is the only one who can meet all conditions, leaving nothing to chance. The unconditional aspect is important because of the tendency in the Christian world to discuss the gift of salvation with only one condition that must be met: faith, or acceptance. If it's stated as a condition that we must meet, though, how will we ever know if we have sincerely accepted Christ, or that our faith is authentic enough? We all know that some days our level of faith is shaky! No, indeed, faith is no condition at all, but rather an encouragement by someone who cares about you—*believe* it! Faith is then an outcome for someone who trusts God's declaration of love for them.

Last, we compared justification to pluripotent stem cells. Just as these stem cells become what they need to be to meet the physiological context, so, too, does justification take the form it needs to disarm the malignant cancer of incurvatus and create wholeness for someone. The effects of sin and brokenness are many and varied, and the good news of justification can take the form of an unconditional promise of forgiveness, or of community, or the affirmation of one's worth (not worthiness!), and so forth. Unless we are justified in a manner corresponding to the form of brokenness within us, we are hopelessly caught up in our self-justifying efforts, and greatly hindered in our capacity to love our neighbor. To be justified is to become free from self in order to love our neighbor. And as we are each justified in a way appropriate to us, we are called to announce the *good* news of justification to others only after listening to what their bad news is first.

Reflection: processing what you've learned

MY OWN LIBERATION

1. Have you ever been in a conversation about a deathbed conversion and wondered if it's fair or not? What do you think of that?

_____

_____

_____

2. Do you think it's a good thing that a person can be unconditionally justified as a gift without having to demonstrate any worthiness? Should Jesus really have to marry a bride with *serious issues*?

_____

_____

_____

3. Do you think it's important to understand the difference between becoming righteous ourselves and trusting in Jesus's "alien" righteousness? Why or why not?

_____

_____

_____

4. Do you see the difference between God's unconditional promise and a conditional one (based on our response)?

_____

_____

_____

5. We talked about different expressions of brokenness, including guilt, shame, meaninglessness, and isolation. Which experiences do you think are most prevalent today? How about for yourself?

_____

_____

_____

6. What does it mean to you that God's love for you is *pluripotent*?

_____

_____

_____

MY NEIGHBOR'S NEED

1. How do the burdens of our brokenness hinder our callings and ability to love our neighbor? Do you see why it is important to have the promise of justification and to be free?

_____

_____

_____

2. If a major part of discernment is listening to and understanding the needs of my neighbor, how does pluripotent love help in our discernment task?

_____

_____

_____

3. What are the needs of my neighbors who are in my life? How might I seek a greater understanding of their needs?

_____

_____

_____

4. What form does love take in me with my neighbors?

_____

_____

_____

Wrap-up

What's one takeaway you have from Chapter 10?

_____

_____

_____

What's one question you have from Chapter 10?

_____

_____

_____

We affirm the Lordship of Christ not in relation to private religion, but over public history ... Our mission is to make a mess of the line that runs between the church and the world, by mixing the gospel into every sector of life.

—Carl Braaten, *The Flaming Center*

CHAPTER 11

THE GIFT OF HOPE: THE KINGDOM OF GOD

Review and reflection

So often faith and religion are rendered as a to-do list for believers to justify themselves before God, as if everything is really in human hands. Or, in modernism and postmodernism, we justify our existence not to God but to self and others. In either case, it's all about what we do, not God. We have misunderstood what it means to be made in the image of God by seeking to be God. We rebelled against our original calling to care for creation and for one another, choosing instead to lean into power, self-interest, and the domination of others. Our attempts at self-justification were futile, and the ensuing disaster led to bondage of the will and a pervasive despair within the soul the human race. The very freedom we sought had become a prison so impenetrable we couldn't turn things around even if we wanted to!

This is why we need a savior. Not only do we need to be saved *from* the meaninglessness of our doomed existence, we need to be saved *for* a whole new existence altogether. Only Christ, by shouldering our brokenness and its consequences, could save us from our bondage of self-justification. Only Christ, by conferring his own goodness to us—thereby justifying us—could save us for a new life. The fact that we can do nothing to accomplish these things makes it abundantly clear that the

Christian faith will be primarily about what God does, not us. Hence, we are justified by grace through faith, as Luther famously asserted. We are called to declare the true nature of freedom to our fellow human beings, namely, that we humans are dependent creatures—dependent on the breath and Word of God for life and restoration.

However, as secondary agents to God's primary agency, God's justification of us has set us free to fear, love, and trust God and love our neighbor. Only God's justification of us as a gift can set us free to engage our callings with a love that seeks the good of the neighbor and the created order. What that world will look like is the focus of Chapter 11.

CHAPTER OVERVIEW

What does it look like when God's promises—and God's second creation—come to fruition and God's will is done? *The kingdom of God.* While a *new creation* is a more cosmic way of putting it, the *kingdom of God* is a more specific image invoked so people can visualize what it looks like in human society when God's reign is complete, when people are reconciled with God and with each other. The fact that the kingdom of God is promised as the outcome of human history creates hope and anticipation that, properly understood, undergirds our callings in a powerful and comprehensive vision. Such a world is grounded in certain values like peace and justice, abundance and gratitude, forgiveness and reconciliation, compassion and love, healing and restoration, community, unity, and inclusivity. The kingdom of God combines both our relationship with God and our relationships with each other. To be reconciled with God necessitates that we will seek to be reconciled with our neighbor and the community of creation in all its diversity. In the kingdom of God, you cannot have one without the other.

Hence, we ought never to excuse ourselves from working to make this world a more just and fair world because we're just biding our time waiting for the next world (second creation) to be fully established. Both the Ten Commandments and our call to bear witness to the kingdom of God demand action and embodiment *now.* Regardless of the urgency of enacting a fairer and more equitable world—one that many outside the Christian tradition share—the fact remains that this world can be a discouraging place when progress is slow or non-existent. The result is often a sense of hopelessness and cynicism about taking action, which is exactly why the promise of the kingdom of God is so significant. It cannot be underestimated how important it is to know how things will end. This not only creates much-needed hope; this very hope is energy for action.

We are called to bear witness to God's kingdom and its values in three ways. First, we bear witness by proclaiming the kingdom of God as the answer and the endpoint of human history! To believe in such a future gives hope, freedom, and direction to us in the present. Second, we witness by taking Jesus's words to heart, "the kingdom of God is at hand" (Mark 1:15). Indeed, Jesus is the embodiment of the kingdom, and so the kingdom does show up in our world in the many incarnations of the body of Christ. We are then called to watch for it, recognize it, and point to it—proclaim it as such! Third, we witness by grounding our lives in the values of the kingdom of God and promoting their practice in our communities—both public and private.

Introduction to *the gift of the kingdom of God*

THE FUTURE AND PIZZA HUT
Of all the animals God made, human beings are uniquely designed to think about the future. As we think about what the future might hold, we approach it with either dread and apprehension, joyful anticipation, or cautious hopefulness. If a person is unable to envision a viable and sustaining future, despair and a pervasive sense of meaninglessness are the inevitable result. This is why hope is so crucial. It speaks to the basic, primordial need of having a future.

Let me share two outdoor experiences that illustrate this. The first one happened when my friend and I, then in our twenties, were leading a group of a dozen or so junior high students on a canoe trip in the Boundary Waters. We were self-guided, had a map, all the necessary gear, and plenty of food, but we did not have campsites reserved. Not sure that was even possible. So, like everyone else, each evening we would have to find an unoccupied campsite. Late one afternoon, I remember paddling many miles and then looking for a campsite. We came upon a few, but they were taken, so we kept paddling. Here was a situation where our immediate future had no guarantees. We were unsure if there was a designated campsite for us or if we would have to set up a makeshift campground in the woods. That evening was uncertain and it was hard to have confidence about what lay ahead. There was nothing promised to us, so there was anxiety. If this is symbolic of your life, the anxiety is probably a lot more serious than looking for a campsite.

Contrast this with another experience, hiking with my youth group in Colorado. We were hiking back to the trailhead after a day of mountain climbing. The night before, we camped at a high mountain lake. Now, on the backside of our outing, our canteens were dry and our food was gone. And since we had expended an incredible amount of energy during these two days, we were really, really hungry and even thirstier. But we knew what was at the end of our trail—our two parked vehicles and the town of Buena Vista. And Buena Vista had a Pizza Hut! We could already taste the pizza and refreshing drinks. Eventually, we arrived and ate large quantities of pizza and quenched our thirst. It was marvelous! It was then that Tom, one of our high school members, said, "I feel like I've died and gone to Pizza Hut!" He perfectly captured our feelings. Indeed, it felt like heaven.

For many today in various ways, hopelessness is a constant companion that destroys the human spirit far more than not finding a campsite one night. My friend who is a pastor in north Minneapolis works closely with the residents of the black community there where poverty, gangs, and unemployment are debilitating problems. He told me recently about his interactions with some of the young men in this community. They spoke of having no hope whatsoever that anyone outside of their neighborhood cares about them. Their plight is experienced as an unavoidable dead end. What does that do to a person when they can envision no positive outcome? When they feel that the extended community of which they are a part cares nothing for them?

Or consider a recent *New York Times* column that examined a phenomenon that researchers have consistently observed for decades. People who are most concerned about social justice and working for change are also less happy and more likely to be depressed than those who are more accepting of the way things are.[1] One might think that those who are passionately engaged in a just cause have found something meaningful to live for. That might be true, but perhaps only if they have a genuine sense of hope that justice was going to be done in the end. But no matter the passion one feels for a just cause, if one feels the situation is hopeless, the future hangs over them like a shroud.

---

1   Edsall, "Happiness Gap."

LEARNING: WITNESSING TO THE KINGDOM OF GOD

The above examples only illustrate the importance of the Christian's calling to bear witness to something that fosters hope. Whether it's a more trivial pursuit—like a Colorado hike—or pursuit of more far-reaching outcomes, we are all hungry and thirsty for that which is fair and just, and signifies abundant life. God promises that our voids and deepest longings will be filled and quenched in the fullness of time. Like my Boundary Waters experience, we need not wonder whether there will be a place for us to stay up ahead on the road of life. God promises a place for us to stay where we belong. No one should have to wonder if they will ever have opportunities for work or a safe neighborhood.

The promises of abundance and belonging are promised by the only one who can make such promises unconditionally: the gracious God who made us and has re-made us in Christ. Never underestimate the power of knowing what lies ahead. For oppressed groups in this world, such a belief in the justice and liberation that lie ahead is a powerful thing. Consider the plight of enslaved African Americans who drew so much strength and hope from the story of God's liberation of the enslaved Hebrew people in the exodus. Without a story of liberation and promise, the specter of hopelessness looms large in a life that is often unjust and can be overwhelmingly oppressive. With the promise of knowing where your story is headed comes hope and meaning in one's current struggle. Efforts at doing what is right are not merely a righteous protest for their own sake, but a witness to what is true and, ultimately, *will come to pass*. This, in turn, lends considerable meaning to one's current struggle.

FILM CLIP

In the movie, *Places in the Heart*, we see a story unfold during the Depression in rural Texas. It is a story of struggle and hardship, racism, infidelity, conflict, and death. In short, this world is a mess, but there is one thing its characters have in common: their faith and the church. While the residents don't necessarily share the same church (or even attend church), there is a vision that concludes the movie, which is nothing short of a glimpse into the kingdom of God. Communion is passed from one person to another, and as the camera moves from one to the next, you quickly realize that something transcendent is happening. All the characters in the film—friends and enemies, wives and mistresses, living and dead, black and white, a blind man who now sees—take communion together at a church service.

This is a scene of great vision and power, because, obviously, in this world we live in, some people with irreconcilable differences and hatred in their hearts wouldn't be caught dead sharing communion. Nor would those who have passed away have been able to turn back the clock. The movie ends with the kingdom of God. What can that mean for our lives in *this* earthly kingdom, knowing where we are headed?[2]

Back to the future!

You might not know exactly when or how, but the outcome—the kingdom of God—is certain. In fact, in the kingdom/new creation is near to you right now, not merely relegated to the distant future. As we have reiterated in this course, we Christians live in two creations. The first one, though it belongs to God, is fallen and broken. We are called to bring love into this world and actively work to co-create with God a more trustworthy world—and a more loving one. As important as our callings are to love our neighbor and co-create a more trustworthy world, these very objectives are shared by most ethical systems and religions. Yet no amount of hard work to make the world more just or trustworthy will save anyone in an ultimate sense or usher in the kingdom in the present. Only God can save us by reconciling our relationship to God. And that is what the second creation is all about.

The kingdom of God is both a new beginning and a new ending. This new creation is based on the fulfillment of the Ten Commandments through Christ, such that our future looks completely different now. In the promised future, humanity will be recreated to love one another and God in such a way that peace, unity, inclusivity, justice, and forgiveness will prevail.

And yet, in this world, such kingdom values seem like an unrealistic dream. The first creation is the world we live in, the one in which it is the survival of the fittest, where Christian ideals of forgiveness, peacemaking, and compassion are often dismissed as naive (and sometimes dangerous) fantasies. Just watch TV shows where survival is often a major part of the plot. Notice how often in these shows it is seen as folly to forgive others or to show compassion to folks who maybe can't be trusted.

---

2 Benton, *Places*, 1:44:42—1:48:05.

It is true that God's promises about the lion lying down with the lamb, swords being beaten into plowshares, and the blind seeing again have not yet fully come to pass. And yet, the future has been set by what the past has given us: Jesus Christ, crucified and risen. Because sin and death have been disarmed forever by Jesus's life, death, and resurrection, the future is certain. All the values of God's kingdom will come to pass. It's all about the future. It can often be said that, in the words of a popular movie, we need to get *back to the future!* It is the promised future that transforms the present on a bedrock of hopefulness and confident resolve.

And so, we proclaim the promised future so that others may be given hope, encouragement and courage to lean into this future with confidence!

The kingdom of God is at hand!

In the Gospel of Mark, Jesus proclaims, "The time is fulfilled, and the kingdom of God has come near; repent, and believe in the good news." (Mark 1:15). In the Gospel of Luke, Jesus instructs his disciples to announce a similar message right before sending them out door to door: "The kingdom of God," says Jesus, "has come near to you." (Luke 10:9). But what does it mean? Simply put, *the kingdom of God is the new creation in Christ*. It is nothing less than a re-ordering of creation characterized by peace, justice, abundant life, and a restored relationship with God.

But why does Jesus say the kingdom has come *near*? Because the kingdom *is* Jesus. Jesus is the embodiment of God's kingdom—a real, live, in-the-flesh, human being to show us what the kingdom looks like. And not only show us. Jesus *is* the new creation, and he's standing right in front of us. That is why Jesus said, "The time is fulfilled;" because Jesus is the fulfillment. And so, the reason the kingdom shapes the present for us is not only because we know how the story ends (which is pretty cool in itself). But also, we have been given a restored relationship with God through Jesus, which creates the conditions for us to embody the kingdom of God, albeit in a very qualified, incomplete sense. And that is true *right now*.

Luther taught that God's incarnation in this world was not a one-time thing, but a decision by God to pitch a tent and remain in the world. God in Christ is present in wine and bread and in those who are baptized into his body. This means God is loose in the world, in our neighborhoods, in our churches, and in our own person. And so, as Christ is present and at work in the world, and Christ is the kingdom of God in the flesh, we can observe expressions of the kingdom right now, even in a fallen world like ours.

For instance, every time we take part in the Lord's Supper, we are acknowledging the existence of another kingdom where everyone who comes forward is equal—that is, equally in need of God's grace and welcome at the table. All the levels of status and importance set by the world are thrown out according to the kingdom's values. The CEO or state judge is no less in need of forgiveness than the bus driver, the cleaning lady, or the ex-con who also ventures forward. Before God, we are all beggars in need of grace.

Alternatively, you might observe two people reconciling with each other. Might this be the kingdom of God happening right in front of you? Then point, and tell someone this is of God! Or perhaps you see lives being transformed by the local AA group, wherein its members learn to admit they are powerless and must submit to a higher power that brings restoration. It may not be the church but is likely an expression of the kingdom of God.

And so, we are called to not only proclaim the kingdom to come, but to announce the kingdom that is present in the world now. We are called to notice, to point, and then to announce, *There it is! Do you see it?*

Last, we are called to participate.

Participating, leaning, and pointing

Because the fulfillment of the kingdom of God is a promise of the future, sometimes we wonder what it has to do with today. As we've already seen, we are participating in the kingdom through Christ, so we know that this kingdom is not only relevant for the next life. And as we see signs of God's kingdom present in the world through Christ and the work of the Holy Spirit, we are not only called to proclaim this and announce it to our neighbors, but to participate, to lean in, to ground our lives in the kingdom values. Leaning means we are intentionally trying to live out kingdom values in our lives, to *be* what we say we believe. So, if the kingdom of God is about peace, about beating swords into plowshares, then that means we are called to reshape our instruments of aggression and fear into means of cultivating sustenance and life. What does that mean for you?

Leaning into the kingdom doesn't just mean privately practicing its values. It also means advocating for their implementation in the public square. It is to believe and respond to our world, knowing where God is heading with humanity! If the kingdom of God unites all nations, what does that mean for how we treat other nations and peoples that are different from ourselves? God is aiming at unity and inclusivity. Are you as well? How do we love and respect those who are *other* and form community with them?

The only qualifier is that in a fallen world such as ours, which is ruled more by law than grace, security and safety dictate that forgiveness is not always possible in public policy and criminal justice. Nor are peace and pacifism always advisable given the magnitude of evil that is loose in the world. Often, much more complicated decisions must be made, as we recognize the stark differences between the two creations and what is possible, good, and right. In some cases, the best choices available in a fallen world are compromises in themselves.

Regardless of where one finds oneself in this fallen world, the one thing that is constant is the call to love, whatever that means for a given situation. One can quickly see that embracing and advocating kingdom values is really nothing other than loving your neighbor as yourself in a complete, proactive, and full manner that is adapted to the context. And then we've come full circle! The Ten Commandments, in the way of life they prescribe, are primarily the work of bearing witness to the coming kingdom of God. And as we've already seen, we are actively participating in the kingdom through Christ, so we know that this kingdom is not only relevant for the next life, but also for this one. So, as we see signs of God's kingdom present in the world, we are not only called to proclaim this and announce it to our neighbors, but to participate, to lean in, and to ground our lives in the values of the kingdom of God.

SUMMARY

The kingdom of God is what human existence looks like when God's will is done. Faith, hope, and love come to fruition and human life flourishes in abundance. The kingdom happens when our relationships with each other and God are brought into seamless alignment. So, this leads to three key ways we bear witness to the kingdom of God. First, we point to its future fulfillment as an anchor for our hopefulness and encouragement in our present dealings. It makes a great deal of difference when we are trudging along life's difficult path to know what is at the end of the trail. This is especially true for those who have been marginalized or oppressed. If the ending is up for grabs, we can easily fall into the grips of meaninglessness. If, on the other hand, we know justice will be done and life will win, our toil has meaning. Second, while we live in a world that is most decidedly *not* the kingdom of God, we also recognize that the kingdom is at hand in Jesus Christ and at work through the power of the Holy Spirit. Thus, we can catch glimpses of God's kingdom in this world and are called to point to it, announce it, and work together for its expression in both the public and private square. Third, we bear witness to the kingdom by living it; by embodying its substance and values in our lives, however imperfectly that might be as we also struggle with our fallen nature. But we are not limited to the expression of kingdom values in our private life, as we are called to be advocates for its expression in public life as well.

Reflection and conversation: processing what you've learned

1. How much anxiety do you have about the future? Which things cause the most anxiety?

_____

_____

_____

2. What does it mean for you that you know how the story ends? Are there promises God makes that give you comfort because you know you can count on them (just like Pizza Hut)?

_____

_____

_____

3. In Jesus, the kingdom of God has been fulfilled and come near to you. How do you think you can become more attentive and open to the kingdom being a part of your life?

_____

_____

_____

KINGDOM VALUES

4. In your own life, how are you already participating in and following kingdom values?

_____

_____

_____

5. How might you lean into kingdom values in new ways and embrace the future in present practice?

_____

_____

_____

6. Where can you point to these values as they are manifest in the world around you?

_____

_____

_____

Take a journey through the following kingdom values and examine how you bear witness to them—by pointing and leaning into them. Make notes for pointing on one side, and leaning on the other side.

1. Peacemaking and reconciliation

    Point to/announce _____

    Lean into/take action _____

2. Inclusivity and diversity

    Point to/announce _____

    Lean into/take action _____

3. Social and economic justice

    Point to/announce _____

    Lean into/take action _____

4. Forgiveness and grace

    Point to/announce _____

    Lean into/take action _____

5. Healing and restoration

    Point to/announce _____

    Lean into/take action _____

6. Abundance and gratitude

    Point to/announce _____

    Lean into/take action _____

7. Love and compassion

Point to/announce _____

Lean into/take action _____

Wrap-up

What questions do you have about Chapter 11?

_____

_____

_____

What takeaways do you have?

_____

_____

_____

An individual is not a person …
A person, unlike an individual, is a human
existence living in the resonant field of his
social connections and his history. He has a
name, with which he can identify himself.
A person is a social being.

—*Jürgen Moltmann, Experiences in Theology*

The future of the church is dependent upon
the hospitality of the world.

—*Patrick Keifert, Missional Church*

CHAPTER 12

THE GIFT OF PARTNERS

Review and reflection

The Lutheran witness has always been rooted in telling it like it is. There is no reason to pretend that we don't live in a deeply compromised world that has, in turn, deeply compromised each of us—in fact, there is good reason *not to* pretend! When humility is lacking in matters of faith, it usually means someone thinks they've arrived and sees things much more clearly than they actually do. Inevitably, this leads to self-righteousness and a less-than-charitable attitude toward the many out there who, in their own estimation, are not as good as they are. It also leads to the naive belief that if enough of us get busy, we can establish the Promised Land right here, right now. This theological journey about callings has invited us to tell the truth about ourselves and our world. To the extent that we are in the driver's seat of our destiny—even with the best of intentions—we make a mess of this world and always will. A significant aspect of that mess is the meaninglessness that we have bequeathed to our children as we have unquestioningly encouraged them (and ourselves) to make a name for themselves or become anything they choose to be. No, we are not gods, and when we think we are, life curves in on itself within us, sharply limiting the reach of our emancipated human capacity while expanding our potential for doomed outcomes. This confession of sin and fallenness is at the root of our understanding of calling, for it is only in a redemptive and dependent relationship with a loving God that we can respond to a calling from God and experience genuine meaning and life-giving purpose. The kingdom of this world—and our own compromised inner and outer life—only reminds us that we cannot save ourselves, but must rely on a savior who promises a new reality for us.

And God did create a new reality, the kingdom of God in a person. God so loves this world that God entered it, loved the least of us, and drank the poison that has cursed this world to death and meaninglessness. Having forged an antidote to sin and death, Christ rose as the first fruit of a new creation and manifestation of the kingdom of God—a creation into which we are all invited. And as members of this kingdom, we bear witness to it in this world. A cynic might say, The new creation is well and good, but what's the point of investing anything in *this* world? But we are not cynics because the promise of the coming kingdom (and new creation) is at hand in the present world and will one day transform it. Hence, we never, ever, give up on the present, fallen world.

Our relationship with God having been restored—as well as our trust in the future—we recognize, as Christians, that our faith is all about what God does, not what we do. And what does God do? God sets us free to fully participate with God, calling us daily to join God in making this world a more trustworthy, hopeful, and loving world. Called daily to point to and lean into the endpoint of human history that is firmly in God's hands.

This dance between the old and new in our world and in ourselves is not easy, however. We need each other for support and help in navigating these two creations at once, in figuring out our callings and how we're doing. We need the mutual conversation and consolation of the saints.

What sticks with you from the last chapter on the "kingdom of God?"

_____

_____

_____

What unresolved questions do you have?

_____

_____

_____

CHAPTER OVERVIEW

Our callings do not occur in a void. They are born and nurtured in community. As we live out our callings as individuals and find our way on our faith journey, all of us need the encouragement, insight, accountability, and feedback that a community of trusted friends can provide. This must be stressed even more so in such a thoroughly individualistic culture as ours, for a community like this is increasingly rare, but is more needed than ever. Furthermore, any Christian community is also called—as a community—to form a missional identity. It is, therefore, critical to learn how to discern as a community. Community, in turn, also has a vital role to play in shaping the callings of individuals.

What is less understood within Christian communities is the importance of forming community with our neighbors outside the confines of our congregation. In the spirit of Luke 10:1-12, we are sent out to find people of peace not only for the sake of mission, but also to encounter the living God in community with our neighbors. Since God is loose in the neighborhood—and at work there—we will find partners in mission in those homes and on those streets. They, too, along with our fellow church members, are gifts to us.

So, in this session, we will explore why forming Christian community is so important for mission. We will also do some basic discernment together using some of our top gifts.

LEARNING: WE REALLY ARE IN THIS THING TOGETHER

Living the called life

In my preface, I shared a conversation I had with a church member (president, actually) who was taken aback at my suggestion that his job as an architect was a calling from God. No, he countered, only pastors and those who have explicitly Christian jobs are called from God, not the vast majority who have non-religious jobs. That, of course, was a sad indictment of pastors and church leadership for not doing a better job communicating a significant teaching of the Reformation, of which we are descendants.

Admittedly, though, for many, the idea that each of us has a calling—several, actually—is a new way of thinking. But it's a whole lot more exciting than just working for a paycheck or volunteering out of a sense of obligation. To be called means you have the gifts to do something that needs to be done. It means that you are in an ongoing relationship with the living God who has summoned you to do something you are uniquely positioned to do. This is faith in action, and it engenders hope because you are an active participant in the missio Dei.

That said, it's not always easy to know what God is calling us to do. And sometimes we will feel that we're not doing very well. To live the called life is to ask a lot of questions: What does God want me to do? What does my calling mean in this or that situation? Why do I sometimes feel I'm not doing a good job with my calling? When it comes right down to it, what *am* I good at?

It is precisely because of these questions that we need each other. Often, we live our our callings privately, in our own world, and yet the called life is not merely a private affair between me and Jesus. Rather, Christian callings come out of and are sustained by community. We need to help each other identify and live out our callings. And when we stumble, we need each other to pick us up and pray for us! And before we can even entertain a possible calling from God, we must have a basic grasp of what our gifts are, but that's not always easy to discern. Sometimes those around us can see what our gifts are better than we can because they have a more detached, objective point of view. Brothers and sisters in Christ—or any friend, for that matter—can be invaluable in giving us a clearer picture of ourselves than we sometimes can.

This is yet another illustration of a theology of the cross at work. Since in this life we "see through the glass darkly," as I Cor 13:12 tells us, we ought not be afraid to admit it. Our broken humanity obscures our vision in life and our ability to discern; we have questions, doubts, and struggles. And all of these elements affect our sense of call. A theology of the cross means we recognize this frequently bumpy road, accept it, and find support and help from our fellow Christians. We don't need to pretend we have our act together all the time—or even once in a while!

The book of Hebrews puts it well, "And let us consider how to provoke one another to love and good deeds, not neglecting to meet together, as is the habit of some, but encouraging one another, and all the more as you see the Day approaching" (Heb 10:24-25).

Practicing community

How do we practice Christian community with one another? Living in Christian community means always wondering what God is doing in our midst, then attempting to discern what that is and how we, as Jesus's followers, are a part of it. This is literally what church means: a people designated as holy who are set apart *from* the world for the very purpose of God's mission *in* the world. A small group that practices discernment and the mutual conversation and consolation of the saints (as discussed earlier) is *being* the church, which is continuously gathered and sent, back and forth. That means our callings are where the rubber meets the road. It's what Christian community is all about.

One of the tasks of the Christian community is cultivating and discerning a *congregational* missional identity. It means asking the same questions about our collective identity that we ask of ourselves as individuals. How are we gifted? Who is our target audience? What should we be doing? What shouldn't we be doing? If a congregation is open to a journey of discovering their identity, they will pay attention to those who are receptive to them in the broader community ("people of peace," as Luke 10:6). They will learn from their experiments about how and why to do mission.

One of the gifts that identity clarification can offer to a community of faith is not having to do everything or be all things to all people. It gives the community permission to say no to some things and concentrate on what they're good at, what they're called to do.

Disruptive and repeatable faith practices

We've established the importance of the gathered community, usually in small groups where discussion can take place about individual and corporate callings. But how do groups go about doing this sort of work? Disruptive faith practices allow communities to practice being church together and discern callings. They are disruptive because they are designed to allow space for the Holy Spirit to disrupt our established patterns of living where we are in control and not always open to the work of the Holy Spirit. These practices are also repeatable—and must be—to be effective. In this respect, they must become habits. What makes faith practices valuable is that they keep us engaged with the above questions. They are the beats that allow us to find the rhythms of the called life.

What follows are the six disruptive practices that Church Innovations discovered in their research that characterize congregations that have learned to be missional in their identity and practice.[1] These six are followed by additional practices that Christian communities have found to be very helpful.

- The practice of *discernment* is trying to listen together to how God is calling us. This is not an exact science (and we'll often get it wrong), and yet there are many considerations and sources one can turn to in the practice of discernment.
- The practice of *giving and receiving hospitality* from one another creates an atmosphere of trust and comfort for sharing our faith journeys with each other, including the living out of our callings.
- The practice of *dwelling in the Word* is a way to listen for God's voice in scripture, the voice that ultimately calls each of us.
- The practice of *bearing witness to the kingdom of God* in the world (or our lives) is a way of paying attention to what God is doing in the world, which helps us locate the nature and place of one's calling.
- The practice of *dwelling in the world* means learning to listen to our neighbors so that we might be attentive to where a calling might suddenly emerge.
- The practice of *planning experiments focusing on mission* as we seek to live out our callings is an excellent community activity that helps us learn about the nature and effectiveness of our callings. But mostly, this practice helps communities gain clarity about their missional identity.

---

1 Keifert, *Change*, 127-34.

- The practice Luther made famous—the *mutual conversation and consolation of the saints*—is the practice of listening to each other and making sense of our life journeys at the high and low points of our lives. This is how we help each other track the ups and downs of our called life.
- The practice of *prayer* means talking and listening to God. This conversation with God is an indispensable practice—out of this conversation a new calling often emerges.
- The practice of *gratitude* means taking time to reflect on those things for which we are grateful. This helps us see the shape of our story through the lens of our assets. This, again, helps shape our sense of calling.
- The practice of *learning* means examining our collective human story, both in the Bible and throughout human history. Anchored in Christian theology, learning means discovering how we can partner with God to create a more trustworthy world and set realistic goals based on our knowledge and exploration.

Forming community with our neighbors

The missional church movement began several decades ago as a response to the suffocating institutionalism and maintenance mindset of Western post-Christendom (post-1965) that has led to steadily decreasing membership in churches. The organizing principle of this movement is based on the observation that the church writ large must adapt to a changing culture that is increasingly pluralistic and indifferent to its existence. This cultural landscape is not unlike that of Mesopotamia at the time of the early church, where engaging in mission and evangelism was its bread-and-butter as it exploded into the Mesopotamian world. I mention the early church because it is quite clear that the contemporary Christian Church must also function missionally not only to survive but to thrive, and, most importantly, to be faithful to its very purpose. We in the church cannot afford to be maintenance-oriented, but must rediscover how to do mission and act with the same sort of resolve and strategy as the early church.

One of the definitive scripture passages for the missional church is Luke 10:1-12, the sending of the seventy. It is an example of how mission was carried out in Jesus's time and is instructive for our time as well.

After this the Lord appointed seventy others and sent them on ahead of him in pairs to every town and place where he himself intended to go. He said to them, 'The harvest is plentiful, but the

201

laborers are few; therefore, ask the Lord of the harvest to send out laborers into his harvest. Go on your way. See, I am sending you out like lambs into the midst of wolves. Carry no purse, no bag, no sandals; and greet no one on the road. Whatever house you enter, first say, "Peace to this house!" And if anyone is there who shares in peace, your peace will rest on that person; but if not, it will return to you. Remain in the same house, eating and drinking whatever they provide, for the laborer deserves to be paid. Do not move about from house to house. Whenever you enter a town and its people welcome you, eat what is set before you; cure the sick who are there, and say to them, "The kingdom of God has come near to you." But whenever you enter a town and they do not welcome you, go out into its streets and say, "Even the dust of your town that clings to our feet, we wipe off in protest against you. Yet know this: the kingdom of God has come near." I tell you, on that day it will be more tolerable for Sodom than for that town.

There are three important elements from Luke 10 that I would like to point out here. First, those who were sent out in mission were not religious professionals, but regular people with various non-religious backgrounds. Luther would say such persons constitute the very priesthood of believers that make up the church. It is the members of a fellowship who are called and sent. It is easy to see the connection with today. All baptized believers have a calling to bear witness to the good news of Jesus Christ.

Second, the future of the faith community Jesus was building was indeed dependent on the hospitality of the surrounding world, namely, neighbors and strangers. It was here that the church was formed, in the encounter of the faithful with the many who were open to the movement of the Holy Spirit. The journey of the early church has striking relevance for today. The future church will be re-formed through the encounter of the faithful with neighbors who, like us, need the good news of Jesus Christ and can become partners in mission with us. This kind of potential for relationships with members of a diverse and pluralistic population again calls to mind the teachings of Luther, who was a strong advocate of our common humanity and membership in the universal church God called forth at the time of creation.

And the reason that followers of Jesus could trust in the strategy of knocking on the doors of strangers is the third point I want to make. As Jesus made clear, his followers could trust his direction because God was already present out in the world as the "Lord of the harvest," whose Spirit of peace had already prepared the hearts and minds of people on the outside of Jesus's fellowship of followers. This means that Jesus was instructing his followers to go into the world to discover where God was already at work, calling them to form community with their neighbors. Remember that our neighbors are not objects for our agendas. Rather, just like us, they are subjects in whom God is at work.[2]

This was the template for Christian mission in the years following Jesus's ascension, and it must be now as well. As theologian and missional church leader Terri Elton suggests, "the church is being called to embrace the role of guest."[3] As we have discussed already, it is a core Lutheran teaching that God is loose in the world creating a trustworthy, hopeful, and loving world. Eugene Peterson has translated Revelation 21:3-4 in *The Message* thus: "God has moved into the neighborhood ..."[4] To speak of God moving into the neighborhood is a modern take on the Lutheran conception of the God who wears masks and is at work in the neighborhood, creating a trustworthy world. One is also mindful of Luther's deeply incarnational theology whereby God is present in all matter and certainly all people, even unbelievers.

As we wind down our examination of how God is calling us, and with whom, it is increasingly clear that those folks outside our circle will be important partners for us—not only to discern what mission looks like in our communities at large, but also because *we need them*. God is there with them, calling us to experience the fullness of our humanity by forming community with the *other*. This is part of leaning into the future, into the kingdom of God in all its universal scope.

In closing, allow me to draw attention to the two threads in this chapter, the community of mutual conversation within the congregation and the community we seek outside the congregation. This dual aspect of community was a lesson I learned as senior pastor at Mt. Olivet Lutheran Church of Plymouth, Minnesota. We were on a three-year journey entitled "Partnership for Missional Church,"[5] a guided journey of missional discovery created by Church Innovations Institute. As we were experimenting with ways that we might form community with members of our neighborhood, we discovered an obstacle to our experimentation: we didn't really know how to form Christian community *within* our congregation. By that I don't simply mean potluck supper community, but community that engages in the disruptive practices discussed earlier. Until we were practicing

---

2 Branson, *Missional Churches*, 38-39.
3 Elton, Journeying, 111.
4 Peterson, *The Message*, 2263.
5 Church Innovations, "Partnership for Missional Church."

community ourselves, how could we form community out in our neighborhood? This led us into a transformational time where we focused on practicing community in both places. In fact, we were called to do so.

SUMMARY

While our callings can be collective, this book has mostly been about discerning individual callings. That said, we are members of a Christian community before we are individual Christians. The body of Christ, as we learned, is a community that depends upon all its members to accomplish its work. So, too, do we as called individuals depend upon that very community of believers to help us discern, engage, and reflect on our callings. Indeed, this is what Luther meant when he held up the importance of the mutual conversation and consolation of the saints. Often, others can help us see ourselves and our possibilities better than we can. It is no mystery that Christ promised to be present in a special way when people are gathered in Jesus's name to consider the matters of faith, callings, and their relationship with God.

We also stressed in this chapter how important it is for us to form community with those beyond the walls of our faith communities, for it is here, too, that God is at work helping people of faith discern what they are called to do and with whom. In fact, as we go out in mission, we will become dependent on the hospitality and community that our neighbors offer us. This is a form of Christian community as God is at work here, planting seeds and reaping the harvest of God's Word in the world. And whereas this can be an individual calling—and certainly does *include* individual callings—the work a faith community is called to in its neighborhood is generally considered a communal calling, discerned by its members in conversation and reflection.

For a faith community to form the kind of meaningful community referenced in this chapter—whether out in the neighborhood or within its own walls—small group gatherings will need to develop disruptive faith practices that invite participants to practice the presence of God together. These practices are keyed by the practice of dwelling in the Word, a relational practice of discernment and listening. Indeed, the task of forming community within the walls of our congregations must go hand in hand with learning to form community with our neighbors.

Reflection and conversation: processing what you've learned

1. Can you name a time when a group of trusted friends/colleagues/ family members/church members helped you see something about yourself or your callings that you previously had not seen?

_____

_____

_____

2. Which of the disruptive faith practices itemized above seems to you to be the most important practice? Why?

_____

_____

_____

3. Which practice appeals to you the most? Why?

_____

_____

_____

4. Which practice seems like it would be the most difficult and perhaps intimidating? Why?

_____

_____

_____

5. How might you facilitate a group of people to venture into the neighborhood to find people of peace and perhaps common ground to form community around a shared mission?

_____

_____

_____

6. What do you think is the missional identity of your faith community? What is your church good at when it comes to bearing witness to the kingdom of God?

_____

_____

_____

TIME FOR DISCERNMENT

What callings have I discerned? What new thing is God seeking to accomplish with and through me? It is time to wonder about the ways I am currently called, both present and pending.

1. When you consider the many gifts that you have, what have you learned about yourself from this course?

_____

_____

_____

2. What callings do you have that you didn't realize were callings before?

_____

_____

_____

3. In light of your gift set, what current activity are you involved in that you may not be called to do? Why? How can you focus your life more, knowing what you have now learned?

_____

_____

_____

4. Looking at your top five spiritual gifts, which one or two are most important to you right now? Why?

_____

_____

_____

5. What might God be calling you to do in your congregation that would utilize that gift? Think outside the box.

_____

_____

_____

If you are doing this course in a class or group, let's practice some communal discernment when we are together.

1. Identify your top five spiritual gifts and share them with your group.

_____

_____

_____

_____

_____

2. Now ask the group to indicate which gift or two the others regularly see in you.

_____

_____

3. Once they've identified these gifts, ask them to brainstorm with you about a few ideas that could take advantage of your gifts and also be missio Dei. Do this for each person.

_____

_____

_____

4. Now discuss how we would go about determining what God is calling us to do _as a faith community_. What things would you look at and consider?

_____

_____

_____

DEVELOPING A PLAN FOR COMMUNITY FOLLOW-UP

How will you make sure you follow up with other like-minded people as you begin to work out your callings—new ones, old ones, emerging ones, fading ones?

_____

_____

_____

I hope this study book has helped you engage in fresh ways with what God might be calling you to do. And I hope it has reinforced for you that God has given each of us meaning and purpose in our lives by virtue of who we are, whose we are, and what we are called to do.

GLOSSARY

Abundance and gratitude: Two terms that remind us that God provides abundantly for all our needs for those who trust God, and even for those who don't! As a result, gratitude is the appropriate response.

Agape **love:** The highest form of love that comes from God is described in the New Testament and embodied by Jesus. This love is based not on feelings or emotions but on a commitment of the spirit and will to speak and act in such a way that the interests of my neighbor are served. Hence, *agape* love is always about my neighbor's needs, not my emotional expression or satisfaction.

Alien righteousness: The Christian teaching that the only kind of righteousness that can save a person from sin and death is a righteousness they do not have. Only an alien righteousness that comes from the outside—from Jesus Christ—can save a person. Living in faith means always clinging to this alien righteousness and not pretending or presuming that it is your own.

Après cinema: The French term for *after* cinema, and a phrase made up by the author. Where *après ski* is the nightlife in a ski town, après cinema is post-movie analysis, usually over a beer or glass of wine.

Baptism: A Christian sacrament celebrating God's promise that we are born anew as members of a new creation. In this rebirth, the old person dies and the new person in Christ is born. It is both a gift to the one born anew and a calling to participate in God's reconciling work in the world.

Bear witness: This means to *point to* the promises of God's faithfulness to us, as well as the kingdom of God and its values. Such witness is a proclamation of the Word of God that brings life.

Body of Christ: Baptized believers who make up the community we call the church together constitute the body of Christ. We are called this because we incarnate the presence of Christ in our gathered community and carry on the continuing mission of Christ in the world.

Calling: Basically, synonymous with vocation. This is a summons by God to you as a baptized believer to participate in missio Dei and be who God made you to be.

Charism/charismata: A gift—or gifts—given to a person by the Holy Spirit, specifically given to a member of Christ's church. The gifts are capacities or skills that one has for building up the church in love and for mission.

Church: Also, the *body of Christ*, the church happens whenever believers are gathered around the living Word of Jesus to share our Lord's sacraments. But that is only the beginning because this gathering is called out into the world with the missio Dei, the mission of God. And so, the church is the church when gathered or sent into the world in many and various configurations.

Conditional: A kind of logic and authority that limits your options moving forward. *If... then...* establishes that if certain conditions are present, then a particular result will follow. *If you overeat, then you will be overweight.* This is how God's law works, as well as the laws of nature. If we do certain things, there will be consequences for me and my neighbor, for better or worse.

Determinism: The philosophical worldview that human agency and freedom are illusions, and that all occurrences in human affairs or otherwise are dictated by outside forces, whether it be God or some mechanistic force like the laws of nature.

Discernment: The practice of listening for God's leading in our lives. Typically, discernment involves many different factors and considerations—like scripture, tradition, experience, personal giftedness, needs of the neighbor, and the still, small voice within, to name a few.

Duty: The experience of being faithful to a calling even when you don't feel like it.

Ekklesia: The Greek word for the church. It means a people called out of the world to serve God in the world.

En Theos: This means *with God*. The word *enthusiasm* comes from this phrase. Perhaps it is the case that our passions have divine origins and are meant to be a way of participating with God.

Equip: To help a baptized believer identify their gifts, discern God's callings to them, and then train and guide that same person in carrying out their callings.

Extrovert: A personality trait whereby one is energized primarily by being around other people and external stimuli.

Father: The first member of the triune God who is best understood as the *will* of God, a will formed by love.

First creation: The creation described in Genesis, where God meant for us to love one another and trust God. It is a broken creation because of the human failure to trust God, and hence, our failure also to love our neighbor. Nonetheless, the first creation is infused with the presence of a loving God working to protect and nurture it.

Gifts of the Spirit: These are the gifts given to members of the church by the Holy Spirit for the sake of equipping its members to build up the body of Christ for its witness in the world.

Gospel: The good news of God's promise to you that through Jesus, God has overcome the forces that destroy our lives: sin, death, and the power of evil. This victory of eternal and abundant life is given freely to all who believe.

Guilt: Either the feeling or the truth (or both) that I have done something (or many things) wrong. Only forgiveness can release us from our guilt.

Healing and restoration: Two terms that indicate God is at work healing human lives and restoring them to wholeness. It is essential to point out that healing and restoration are completed only in death. This is the theology of the cross pushback to theologies of glory.

Holy Spirit: The third member of the triune God, who is best understood as the *power* of God.

Incurvatus se: A Latin word that the church fathers used to describe sin, namely, a life increasingly lived *curved in* on itself and away from God and other people.

Introvert: A personality trait whereby one is energized primarily by their inner life of thought, reflection, and internal stimuli.

Jesus Christ: The second member of the triune God, who is the Son, the *embodiment* of God.

Journey theology: A theology asserting that we work out our relationship with God on a journey of discovery, often not knowing the answers, but open to learning and finding answers along the way. We do this in the company of other travelers who help us find our way. We journey by faith in the ongoing presence of God's Holy Spirit with us and in God's Son, who knows all about earthly journeys. A theology of the cross is a journey theology.

Joyful exchange: Luther's description of how God atones for our sins through Jesus and saves us. In Jesus, God shared his eternal life with humans in exchange for our brokenness, sin, and death. The result is that God bears our brokenness on our behalf, while we receive the life of God.

Justification: Having a right relationship with God, being reconciled with God. More broadly, justification is God's unconditional gift of wholeness and release from all the manifestations of brokenness and sin. For Christians, God alone can justify us, even as misguided human beings find countless ways to try and justify themselves.

Kingdom of God: A biblical term that describes the reign of God when it comes to full fruition. It is a more specific way of talking about the second—or new—creation. The kingdom of God became fully embodied in Jesus of Nazareth and will one day become fully realized for all of us who are in Christ.

Kingdom values: The prominent moral and spiritual characteristics that define the kingdom of God and who Christians are.

Law: God's expectations of us that are conditional by nature and reflect the world God has made. If we are obedient to God's laws, our neighbor will be far better off and our lives will be grounded and generally flourish. If we are not obedient—say for instance, we are unfaithful in our relationships—there will be consequences both for me and for those around me to deal with. God's law, and the world of conditions and laws, are all good, but they cannot save us!

Living Word: The living Word is the most important form the Word of God takes, namely, *Christ*, who became incarnate and dwelled among us. The Word is also spoken as proclamation from believer to listener. It is also printed in the Bible.

Mask: A term Luther used to describe how God hides in the world, wearing masks, while working through people and institutions in public and private spheres to create a trustworthy and loving world.

Missio Dei: A Latin term meaning the *mission of God*. This mission encompasses all that God is up to in the world, which would include protecting and nourishing God's creation, creating a more trustworthy world where life can flourish, saving and redeeming lost lives, and working toward the establishment of the kingdom of God.

Movement: An accurate way to describe the church is *movement*. The church is something that happens, not something stationary. The reason? It is part of God's life-giving movement in the world.

Mutual conversation and consolation of the saints: A phrase coined by Martin Luther to indicate the importance of fellow Christians gathering to reflect on their journeys together, identifying God's presence in those journeys, proclaiming the gospel good news to one another, bearing one another's burdens, and discerning God's leading for tomorrow.

Natural law: This is the moral law that is built into creation as surely as physical laws like photosynthesis. The Ten Commandments, for instance, are a good example of natural law. Their admonitions to love your neighbor prescribe universally agreed-upon principles.

Panentheism: Literally, this means *all* (pan)-*in* (en)-*God* (theism). God is in all things, in all of creation, but also stands apart from creation and is transcendent to creation.

Passions: Those pursuits or activities about which you are highly motivated, either because you really like doing them or you are convicted of their importance. One way or another, what you are passionate about really matters to you, gets you fired up, and comes from your heart.

Peacemaking and reconciliation: Two terms that reveal how it is that God intends to order human society, namely, by cultivating life and wholeness, reconciling conflicts among people, and dismantling aggression against one another.

Performative: The quality of God's speech—the Word—that performs what it declares in the moment it is spoken, as opposed to merely describing something or declaring something that will happen. A performative word is a powerful word!

Perichoresis: An ancient Greek understanding of the triune God that emphasizes the community and inter-relatedness of the persons of the Trinity. This inter-relatedness is sometimes characterized as a dance—a dynamic community in motion with a purpose. Christians believe we have been made members of Perichoresis, not because we've become God too, but because God has chosen to make us members of God's family and promised belonging to us that can never be taken away.

Persona: The personality mask that is put on by someone who is adapting to a social situation. The mask may or may not be a legitimate variant of one's true personality.

Practical atheism: Believing in God but living as though there is no God who is active in our world.

Priesthood of all believers: Luther coined this term, asserting that the work that lay people do in their lives, the places (stations) they occupy, the roles they fill as parents/neighbors/citizens/coworkers, and the like are all callings from God. These callings are as important (or even more so in the case of callings to one's family) as the callings within the church.

Process theology: A theology that asserts that God is in process with us, working in real-time with us to move forward and bring good outcomes out of bad situations. This is a counter-narrative to the *master plan* or deterministic theology.

Promise: The basis of how God gives us life is unconditional promise, the unwavering faithfulness of God to God's children that creates faith and gives life. This is where salvation is found—and it is all God's doing!

Reconciliation: To restore a right relationship between God and humans.

Redemption: God showing up and claiming broken and sinful human beings as God's own, in order to create a new narrative of life out of the very stuff of our brokenness, thereby redeeming us. Salvation

Resurrection: The completion of Christ's victory over sin, death, and the power of evil. In rising to new life, Jesus began a new creation, which is promised to us.

Sacrament: A physical means by which God administers God's grace, promise, and presence to us. For Lutherans, it includes baptism and communion.

Sacred: A place or thing where God is present and at work. Hence, we can say a place has spiritual significance—it is holy ground.

Saints: Baptized believers in Jesus Christ and the triune God. Unlike the Roman Catholic Church, where sainthood holds a special distinction for the truly extraordinary and holy among us, the Protestant notion of sainthood stresses that God is at work in powerful ways in every baptized believer, in the *ordinary*.

Salvation: To be in a right relationship with God and reborn to a hopeful future whereby one is freed from the forces of sin, death, and evil.

Second creation: The new creation in Jesus Christ wherein God reconciles humankind to Godself and unites all creation in Christ. Reconciliation happens through God's promises and the response of faith. This creation is both a reboot and a fulfillment of God's original intentions for creation. The new, second, creation is also another term for the kingdom of God.

Secular: A space, person, or thing devoid of anything divine or godly, and lacking in spiritual substance or significance; usually interchangeable with *ordinary*. Also, a space declared to be free of God's influence or the influence of religion.

Shame: The feeling that your whole person is deficient or wrong. The problem is not something I *did*, it's who I *am*.

Sin: The illusion that we don't need God. All we need are the instructions, and then we'll be fine on our own. Or maybe we'll make our own instructions. Either way is a disaster.

Social and economic justice: Two terms that establish God's solidarity with those who are taken advantage of in the social, economic, and legal structures of this world. Often, but not always, such folks are those without power who live at the margins of society. In God's reign, all are treated fairly and justly, so that everyone has what they need to live in wholeness.

Ten Commandments: God's law given to the Israelites to help them restrain sin, love God, and love their neighbor. It expresses the intent of God for human existence, even as it fails to give life to a humanity in captivity to sin. Instead, the Commandments accuse us and remind us of our sin while at the same time offering the basis for law and duty in a broken world.

Theology of the cross: A theological framework—*theologia crucis* in Latin—coined by Luther that reveals the heart and mission of God, namely, to affirm God's creation and show absolute solidarity with broken human existence, even fully absorbing the worst sinful compulsions of humanity and death itself in order to save us through a new creation. *Theologica crucis* also reveals the condition of humanity in full revolt against God and therefore shows us the only way to life is through death. Finally, this theology establishes God's ongoing mission to seek the marginalized and lost to restore them to community with God and one another.

Unconditional: A kind of logic and authority that states a conclusion and requires no further conditions for its fruition. *Because... therefore...* is how God's promises are framed to us. *Because* God loves you and will go to any length to save you, *therefore* God has defeated all forms of bondage that destroy and limit the experience of true life.

Unity and inclusivity: Two terms that describe the universality of God's reign that will unite all peoples of the earth and include those who are often at the margins.

Values: The guiding principles that give your life meaning, integrity, and direction. In addition, values can give us congruency with our personal identity. Ultimately, only meta-values that turn us away from self to serve the needs of the world are sustaining and in alignment with Christian faith.

Vocation: A term used by Luther and the reformers signifying God's calling to every baptized Christian to do God's work every day at their stations of life. This was a counterproposal to the Roman view that every-day life held few prospects for doing God's work. For them, it was done in churches and monasteries.

Volunteering: Choosing to help without pay, but is only a small fraction of what we mean by a "calling."

Word: First and foremost, the Word is the second member of the triune God—Christ—that became flesh and dwells among us. More than that, the Word is the capacity of God to speak life into existence through either law or promise. Furthermore, this Word speaks through the faithful and is written in scripture.

BIBLIOGRAPHY

Albano, Dominick. "What Is Mary's Myers-Briggs?" *The Catholic Telegraph*, Apr 29, 2022.
https://www.thecatholictelegraph.com/what-is-marys-myers-briggs/80806.

Allen, Woody, dir. *Annie Hall*. New York: A. Jack Rollins and Charles H. Joffe Productions: 1977. https://ok.ru/video/330781887224.

America, In, and Evangelical Lutheran Church of Canada. *Evangelical Lutheran Worship*. Minneapolis: Augsburg Fortress, 2006.

Bayer, Oswald. *Martin Luther's Theology: A Contemporary Interpretation*. Grand Rapids: Eerdmans, 2008.

Benton, Robert, dir. *Nobody's Fool*. New York: Arlene Donovan, Scott Rudin, 1994. DVD.

———. *Places in the Heart*. Alameda, CA: Delphi II Productions, 1984. Sony streaming on Xfinity.

Beresford, Bruce, directors. *Tender Mercies*. London: EMI Films, 1983. https://www.amazon.com/gp/video/detail/0LCOF7O8NH459R2H2I6838P8Q4/ref=atv_dl_rdr?tag=justus1ktp-20.

Braaten, Carl E. *Principles of Lutheran Theology*. Philadelphia: Fortress, 1983.

Branson, Mark Lau, and Nicholas Warnes, ed. *Starting Missional Churches: Life with God in the Neighborhood*. Downers Grove, IL: IVP, 2014.

Brown, C Brené. *I Thought It Was Just Me: Women Reclaiming Power and Courage in a Culture of Shame*. New York: Gotham, 2007.

Cain, Susan. *Quiet: The Power of Introverts in a World That Can't Stop Talking*. New York: Broadway, 2013, 2014.

Chin, Jimmy, and Elizabeth Chai Vasarhelyi, dirs., *Nyad*. Los Gatos, CA: Netflix, 2023.

"CliftonStrengths." Gallup. https://www.gallup.com/cliftonstrengths/en/home.aspx.

Docter, Pete, dir. *Inside Out*. Los Angeles, CA: Walt Disney Pictures, Pixar Animation Studios, 2015. DVD.

Edsall, Thomas. "The Happiness Gap between Left and Right Isn't Closing." *New York Times*, May 8, 2024.

"Enthusiasm." Online Etymology Dictionary. https://www.etymonline.com/word/enthusiasm#etymonline_v_8730.

"Erich Fromm Quotes." Brainyquote. https://www.brainyquote.com/authors/erich-fromm-quotes.

"Extract from the Declaration of Independence, as Adopted by Congress." Tjrs. monticello.org. https://tjrs.monticello.org/letter/1682#.

Fincher, David, dir. *The Social Network*. Los Angeles, CA: Columbia Pictures, 2010. https://www.youtube.com/watch?v=bupOXE5nFDE&t=6840s.

Fleming, Victor, dir. *The Wizard of Oz*. Los Angeles, CA: Metro-Goldwyn-Mayer, 1939. https://archive.org/details/the-wizard-of-oz-1080p.

Forde, Gerhard. *On Being a Theologian of the Cross*. Grand Rapids, MI: Eerdmans, 1997.

"Free Personality Test." 16 Personalities. https://www.16personalities.com/free-personality-test.

"The Enneagram Personality Test." Truity.com. https://www.truity.com/test/enneagram-personality-test.

Gallup, Inc. 2019. "StrengthsFinder 2.0." Gallup.com. 2019. https://www.gallup.com/cliftonstrengths/en/254033/strengthsfinder.aspx.

Gilligan, Vince, Peter Gould, creators. *Better Call Saul*. Producers Bob Odenkirk, Nina Jack, Diane Mercer, Robin Sweet, Gordon Smith, Jonathan Glatzer. AMC Network, 2015-2022.

Gritsch, Eric W., and Robert W. Jenson. *Lutheranism: The Theological Movement and Its Confessional Writings*. Philadelphia: Fortress, 1976.

Haemig, Mary Jane. *Lecture on Lutheran* Confessions. St. Paul, MN: Luther Seminary. 2016.

Haidt, Jonathan. *The Righteous Mind: Why Good People Are Divided by Politics and Religion*. New York: Vintage. 2012.

Hall, Douglas John. *The Cross in Our Context: Jesus and the Suffering World*. Minneapolis: Fortress, 2003.

———. *Lighten Our Darkness: Towards an Indigenous Theology of the Cross*. Lima, OH: Academic Renewal, 2001.

"Holland Code (RIASEC) Career Interests and Myers-Briggs Types." Personalityjunkie.com. https://personalityjunkie.com/holland-code-riasec-career-interests-myers-briggs-types.

Harper, Douglas. 2015. "Online Etymology Dictionary." Etymonline.com. 2015. https://www.etymonline.com/search?q=enthusiasm.

Hudson, Hugh, dir. *Chariots of Fire*. London: Allied Stars Film Limited, Los Angeles: Enigma Productions, 1981. DVD.

Jackson, Peter, dir. *The Lord of the Rings: The Fellowship of the Ring*. Los Angeles: New Line Cinema. Wellington, New Zealand: Wingnut Films, 2001. HBO Max streaming on Xfinity.

Joffé, Roland, dir. *The Mission*. London and New York: Goldcrest Films, 1986. WB streaming on Xfinity.

Johnson, Mark Steven, dir. *Simon Birch*. Los Angeles: Hollywood Pictures, Caravan Pictures, Roger Birnbaum Productions, Laurence Mark Productions, 1998. DVD.

Kazan, Elia, dir. *On the Waterfront*. Los Angeles: Horizon Pictures, 1954. DVD.

Keifert, Patrick R. *How Change Comes to Your Church: A Guidebook for Church Innovations*. Grand Rapids: Eerdmans, 2019.

————. *We Are Here Now: A New Missional Era, a Missional Journey of Spiritual Discovery*. Eagle, ID: Allelon, 2006.

————. *Talking About Our Faith: A Book for Mentoring Conversations*. St. Paul: Church Innovations, 1997.

Kise Jane A. G., David Stark, and Sandra Krebs Hirsch. *LifeKeys Discovery Workbook*. Minneapolis, MN: Bethany House, a division of Baker. 1998, 2005.

Kolb, Robert, and Charles P. Arand. *The Genius of Luther's Theology: A Wittenberg Way of Thinking for the Contemporary Church*. Grand Rapids, MI: Baker Academic, 2008.

Kolb, Robert, and Wengert, Timothy J. Wengert, eds. *The Book of Concord: The Confessions of the Evangelical Lutheran Church*. Minneapolis: Augsburg, 2000.

Kurosawa, Akira, dir. *Ikiru*. Tokyo: Toho Company: 1952. DVD.

"Lao Tzu Quotes." Brainyquote. https://www.brainyquote.com/authors/lao-tzu-quotes.

Linklater, Richard, dir. *School of Rock*. New York: Scott Rudin Productions. 2003. DVD.

Linman, Jonathan. "An Understanding of Mutual Conversation and Consolation and Other Practices that Complement This Means of Grace." Mnys.org. https://www.mnys.org/assets/1/6/mutualconversationandconsolationsummary.pdf.

Luther, Martin. *A Contemporary Translation of Luther's Small Catechism*. Augsburg, 1996. 16.

Martinson Elton, Terri. *Journeying in the Wilderness*. St. Paul: Word & World, 2020.

McCarthy, Tom, dir. *Spotlight*. Beverly Hills, CA: Participant Media. New York: First Look Media, 2015. HBO Max streaming on Xfinity.

"Myers-Briggs Type Indicator." Wikipedia. Last updated 2019. https://en.wikipedia.org/wiki/Myers%E2%80%93Briggs_Type_Indicator.

The New Interpreter's Bible Commentary. Volume 1, Introduction to the Pentateuch, Genesis, Exodus, Leviticus, Numbers, Deuteronomy, 33-40. Nashville: Abingdon. 2015.

The New Interpreter's Bible Commentary. Volume 9, Acts, Introduction to Epistolary Literature, Romans, 1 & 2 Corinthians, Galatians, 814-818. Nashville: Abingdon. 2015.

"Partnership for Missional Church." Church Innovations Institute. https://www.churchinnovations.org/Partnership-for-Missional-Church.

"Personal Values Assessment." https://www.valuescentre.com/pva.

"Personal Values Free Online Test." https://personalvalu.es/personal-values-test.

Peterson, Eugene H. *The Message: The New Testament in Contemporary Language*. Colorado Springs, CO: Navpress, 2003.

Rath, Tom. *StrengthsFinder 2.0 from Gallup: Discover your Cliftonstrengths*. New York: Gallup, 2021.

Robbins, Jerome, and Wise, Robert, directors. *West Side Story*. Los Angeles, CA: Mirisch Pictures, Seven Arts Productions, 1961. DVD.

Schuurman, Douglas James. *Vocation: Discerning Our Callings in Life*. Grand Rapids: Eerdmans, 2004.

Simpson, Gary Dr. "Missional Congregations as Public Companions with God in Global Civil Society: Vocational Imagination and Spiritual Presence." *Dialog* 54, no. 2 (2015) 135–50.

———. "'Putting on the Neighbor': The Ciceronian Impulse in Luther's Christian Approach to Practical Reason." In *The Devil`s Whore: Reason and Philosophy in the Lutheran Tradition*, edited by Jennifer Hockenbery Dragseth. Minneapolis: Fortress, (2014) 31-38.

———. "Thinking with Luther About Jesus: (A.k.a. Sweetlips)." *Word and World* 32, no. 4 (2012) 364-72.

———. "A Reformation Is a Terrible Thing to Waste: A Promising Theology for an Emerging Missional Church." In *The Missional Church in Context: Helping Congregations Develop Contextual Ministry*, Missional Church Series, edited by Craig Van Gelder, 65-93. Grand Rapids, MI: William B. Eerdmans, 2007.

Strommen, Merton P., and A. Irene Strommen. *The Five Cries of Grief: Our Family's Journey to Healing after the Tragic Death of a Son*. Minneapolis: Augsburg, 1996.

Wengert, Timothy J. *Martin Luther's Catechisms: Forming the Faith*. Minneapolis: Fortress, 2009.

Westhelle, Vítor. *Transfiguring Luther: The Planetary Promise of Luther's Theology*. Eugene, OR: Cascade, 2016.

Wingren, Gustaf. *Luther On Vocation*. Evansville, IN: Ballast, 1999.

Zscheile, Dwight J. *The Agile Church: Spirit-Led Innovation in an Uncertain Age*. New York: Morehouse, 2014.

www.ingramcontent.com/pod-product-compliance
Lightning Source LLC
Chambersburg PA
CBHW060333100426
42812CB00003B/974